THE GATES OF FREEDOM

BOOK 3

LOUIS MARKOS
ILLUSTRATED BY ANGELA MERKLE

LAMPION
House Publishing

LAMPION HOUSE PUBLISHING LLC
Navasota, Texas 77868

2025

The Gates of Freedom
Copyright © 2024 Louis Markos

No part of this book may be reproduced in any form or by any electronic or mechanical means including information storage and retrieval systems, without permission in writing from the author. The only exception is by a reviewer, who may quote short excerpts in a review.

Lampion House Publishing LLC
P.O. Box 1295
Navasota, TX 77868
Website: http://lampionhousepublishing.com/

ISBN: 979-8-9918278-2-9 (softcover)

First Edition, May 2025

Cover illustration by Angela Merkle

Cover design by Amy Cole, JPL Design Solutions

Interior formatting by Vickie Swisher, Studio 20|20

Printed in the United States of America

For Dale Olson and Lan Nguyen

Whose encouragement,

counsel, and advocacy

Helped usher me back through

the gates of freedom

BOOK 3: THE GATES OF FREEDOM

PART ONE: LAYING THE CORNERSTONE

Chapter 1: Remember the Alamo 3
Chapter 2: Forgetting 11
Chapter 3: The Sounds of Battle 15
Chapter 4: The First Alamo 23
Chapter 5: A Crisis of Faith 29
Chapter 6: The Trial 35
Chapter 7: The Founding Father 47
Chapter 8: The Chosen 57
Chapter 9: The Rabble-rouser 65
Chapter 10: The Regicides 77

PART TWO: EAST VERSUS WEST

Chapter 11: In the Palace of Darius 93
Chapter 12: Look to the End 99
Chapter 13: The Magi 111
Chapter 14: The Invasion 119
Chapter 15: The Marathon Runner 127
Chapter 16: The Oracle 139

Chapter 17: An Unlikely Savior 149
Chapter 18: In the Court of Xerxes 157

PART THREE: MALE AND FEMALE

Chapter 19: On the Road to War 169
Chapter 20: The New Bride 181
Chapter 21: The True Path.. 189
Chapter 22: A Snake in the Grass 195
Chapter 23: The Three-hundred Spartans 205
Chapter 24: For Such a Time as This.................................. 213
Chapter 25: Leonidas's Last Stand 221
Chapter 26: The Tables Turned 233
Chapter 27: The Wooden Walls 241
Chapter 28: The Golden Age 253

About the Author 259
About the Illustrator 261

— Part —
1

Laying the Cornerstone

*"I gave the people as much privilege as they had a right to:
Neither did I degrade them nor give them too free a hand;
Neither did I give them excessive freedom
nor did I restrain them overmuch."*
—Solon

Chapter

1

Remember the Alamo

For the third time that afternoon, Alex and Stacey looked at each other, burst into a double grin, and began to sing, at the top of their lungs, "The Ballad of Davy Crockett." For you see, Alex had just graduated from fifth grade, and, to celebrate, his family had decided to spend the weekend in a city Alex had always wanted to visit. They had left Houston that morning at 11:30 (Daddy wasn't much of a morning person!), and they were now less than an hour away from their longed-for destination: San Antonio.

San Antonio!

The very name was magical, like one of those secret passwords that opens hidden doors on the sides of ancient hills. Speak it once, and the hills begin to shake; speak it twice, and the rocks are ripped apart, revealing within wonders untold: buried treasure, mysteries forgotten, adventures perilous.

San Antonio! When you whispered it to yourself, it sent a shiver down your spine; when you said it aloud, each syllable seemed to hover for a moment on the air.

"Alright, kids, alright," laughed Daddy, as Alex and Stacey finished the third verse of "The Ballad of Davy Crockett" and started up on the fourth, "I think that's enough singing for now. We'll be there pretty soon, and you don't want to tire yourselves out."

"OK, Daddy," said Alex, "but we'll only stop singing if you tell us the story of Davy Crockett and the Alamo."

"Again!" said Daddy. "Didn't I tell you the story last night before you went to bed?"

"Well, yes," admitted Alex, "but that doesn't mean you can't tell it again."

"Yes, Daddy, yes," chimed in Stacey, "We want to hear it again."

"Alright," said Daddy, "It is one of my favorite stories after all, and before the sun sets tonight you two will be standing in the very spot where Davy Crockett fought and died for the freedom of Texas. I guess that makes the story worth telling again. But first I have some questions for you two. Six different flags have flown over Texas: name the flags and then tell me which one was flying when Davy left Tennessee and headed for Texas."

"I know," said Alex, "I know! First there was the French flag, then the Spanish, and then the Mexican. After that, Texas became her own Republic and flew her own Lone Star flag. Next was the

Confederate flag when Texas joined the South in the Civil War, and the last one was the American flag. By the time Davy arrived at the Alamo, the Mexicans had chased out the Spanish and were in control of Texas."

"Very good, Alex," said Daddy, "I think you should just skip middle school and go right on to high school."

"Why not go right to college, Daddy?"

"Not a bad idea, son, not a bad idea. But can you tell me who the leader of Mexico was?"

"Of course I can," said Alex. "His name was Santa Anna. I know that he was the bad guy and that he was even a bit of a tyrant, but it seems to me he was a pretty good leader."

"Right you are, Alex. He was a great general; he even liked to call himself the Napoleon of the West. But he made one mistake. He underestimated the courage of the Texans. He thought if he marched into Texas with his troops and took over all their cannons and forts that they would surrender and give up their weapons. But he was dead wrong. The Texans had gotten a taste of freedom, and they weren't going to give up without a fight. When Santa Anna told them to surrender one of their cannons, they answered back: 'Come and get it!' They …"

"Hey," cut in Stacey, who was getting a bit impatient, "When do I get to answer a question?"

"OK, Stacey," said Daddy, "OK. Why don't you tell us what the Alamo was."

"That's easy. The Alamo used to be a mission run by Spanish missionaries. They taught the Bible to the Indians, and the missionaries and the Indians all lived and worked together. The mission was big and had walls running all around it for protection. But when Davy came to Texas, it wasn't a mission anymore. The

Mexican army had been using it as a fort until the Texans took it away from them."

"I'm impressed, Stacey," said Daddy, "Maybe you should skip fifth grade and graduate with your brother!"

"Hey, wait a minute," shouted Alex.

"Yes, yes," said Stacey, at the same time, "that's a great idea."

"Alright, alright, settle down back there. Alex, it's your turn. Tell us what troops were stationed at the Alamo and who was in charge."

"Well," said Alex, "some of the troops were Americans who had settled in Texas and some were Mexicans who had also settled in Texas. But the ones I like the best were the soldiers from Tennessee and Kentucky and other states who had come all the way to Texas to help her fight for independence. Davy was one of those! When he got there—in 1836, I think—there were two colonels in charge: William Travis and Jim Bowie. But before the fighting started, Jim Bowie got sick and Travis took charge. It's a good thing Davy came when he did, because Travis needed all the help he could get."

"Excellent," said Daddy, "Now the next question is …"

"No more questions!" shouted Alex and Stacey together, "*You* tell us the rest."

"Very well," said Daddy, "To begin with, you are exactly right, Alex. The year was 1836, and the month was February. Only a few months earlier Texas had declared her right to break away from Mexico and had chosen Sam Houston to lead her rag-tag army. But on February 23, when Santa Anna's troops surrounded the Alamo and laid siege to it, Houston's army was far away. For twelve long days, the Mexican army shot their cannons at the thick walls of the Alamo; for twelve longer nights, the sleepless, ever vigilant Texans repaired the breeches in the wall. Several times, a brave Texan on horseback would charge out of the Alamo and through the enemy lines of the Mexican army. Off he would ride in search of Sam Houston and the Texas army, bearing anxious letters from Colonel Travis. But in the end, no help came. They would have to face the enemy alone.

"Very early on the morning of March 6, 1836, while the Texans lay sleeping in the Alamo, Santa Anna called his troops to order. It was to be a sneak attack, with several different detachments attacking the Alamo from several different points. But his men lost their discipline for a moment, and the sound awoke the sleeping Texans. Immediately they sprang to arms. The day had come when they would show the full valor of their heroic hearts. Though many of them had been Texans for less than a month, they had taken her cause as their own. In the furnace of war they had been forged into a single, mighty sword. They would neither surrender nor desert their post. They would fight to the end whether or not Sam Houston sent them fresh troops. They would all stay true to Davy Crockett's great motto—"

"I know what it was," broke in Alex, who had learned Davy's motto two years earlier in his Cub Scout troupe, "I know! 'Be sure you are right; then go ahead.' That's what Davy always said."

"Right you are, Alex, and that's as good a proverb to live by as any ever spoken. Those men at the Alamo believed that their cause was just. They believed that freedom was worth dying for, and they would prove it on that terrible, bloody morning. For the first few hours, the defenders of the Alamo—outnumbered, outflanked, and outgunned—held back the invading army with some of the sharpest shooting and craziest courage you ever saw. There was really no way that they could win the battle. The walls of the Alamo were just not that high, and there were just not enough men to defend all of the walls at the same time. Still, they fought on. They would show the Mexican army—and the Texas army too—what it meant to be a Texan. They had drawn their line in the sand, and anyone who dared to cross it would do so at great cost.

"Miraculously, they fought back the first wave, but when Santa Anna followed this with a second, stronger attack manned by fresh troops, the Texans knew that all was lost. Swiftly, unstoppably, the Mexican army poured over the walls, pushing the Texans back into the weaker, inner walls of the Alamo. The first to fall was Colonel Travis. Soon after, the conquering army burst into the room where Jim Bowie lay on his sickbed. Swinging his Bowie knife wildly in the air, he held them back for a moment, but he was too weak to hold them back for long. And Davy Crockett? Well, no one knows for sure how he died that day, but I can see him in my mind's eye, charging headlong at the Mexican army. His coonskin hat is fluttering in the breeze, and he is grinning all the time. Even when the bullet rips through his chest and enters his heart, he still thinks to himself that it was right for him to come to Texas … that the cause was just … that the battle was worth fighting."

"But was it worth it?" asked Alex.

"It was indeed," answered Daddy, "Though the battle was lost, and though every soldier perished that day in the fighting, the War for Texas Independence was won. Travis and Davy and all the other defenders of the Alamo slowed down the Mexican army just long enough to give Sam Houston the time he needed to ready his troops for battle. Just as important, the courage they showed in the face of death rallied the hearts and souls of

Texans across the state. 'Remember the Alamo,' they cried, and with that as their motto, they swept down on Santa Anna and his troops, defeating them for good at the battle of San Jacinto. Was it worth it? I'll say it was. That's why, even though San Jacinto is much closer to Houston than San Antonio, we've chosen to head straight for the Alamo."

"No, Daddy," said Alex," that's not what I mean. I'm not asking you *was* it worth it. What I want to know is was *it* worth it. Freedom, I mean. Is freedom *really* worth dying for? What's so important about freedom? Haven't we always been free? I mean, in school they're always telling us that we have freedom of speech and that everyone can vote, but is that stuff really worth dying for?"

"That's a good question, Alex, and an important one. To answer it, we need to go way back to the beginning, to the foundations of freedom, to ancient Israel and ancient Greece—"

But that's as far as Daddy got. Mommy, you see, was the type of person who was always worried about getting lost, and so, as soon as she noticed a bunch of street signs announcing that they had just entered San Antonio, she told everyone in the car that they must all be quiet so that she could find the sign that would direct them to their hotel.

Santa Anna had nothing on Mommy; all three Texans stopped talking immediately!

Chapter

2

Forgetting

The Alamo was even more wonderful than Alex and Stacey had imagined. Though much of the long, circular wall that had once surrounded the mission was gone, there was still enough of it left to give the children a sense of what the battle must have been like. Even better, the fact that so much of it had crumbled away and that only portions of it were left made it seem much, much older than it actually was. In reality, the battle of the Alamo was fought less than 200 years ago and the mission itself had been built less than 200 years before that, but as Alex and Stacey gazed on the remains of the Alamo, it seemed to them like one of the many ruins they had seen three years earlier when they had visited Greece with their mother. That, of course, was during that magical summer when the two children had been drawn back, by the power of the dreaming stone and a set of panpipes, into the world of Greek mythology.

What a summer that had been! While their school friends were swimming at the community pool and riding their bikes, Alex and Stacey were helping Perseus to kill the dreaded Medusa, accompanying Orpheus to the Underworld, and fighting the Minotaur with that most noble of heroes, Theseus. And if that were not adventure enough for a lifetime, when the next summer rolled around, Alex and Stacey were taken back once again to ancient Greece where they met the mighty heroes of the Trojan War and the beautiful women who loved and suffered for them. Though Alex was only nine at the time and Stacey only eight, they had both shown great courage and faith: in the face of a hidden, but deadly evil, they had not only taught Achilles to put away his wrath but had helped to reunite the loyal family of Odysseus. And by so doing, they had, wonder of wonders, helped to save civilization itself!

Well, as you might imagine, when the next summer arrived, Alex and Stacey were half expecting that they would be drawn back again into the misty world of Greek mythology. Indeed, every time they peered over the top of a hill or opened a rusty door or strained their eyes to see the end of a rainbow, they were sure, *quite* sure, that Pan or Theseus or maybe even Zeus himself would appear out of nowhere and invite them back into the land of legends. The world was full of magic, their Daddy had taught them: they just needed eyes to see it and ears to hear it—and a nose to smell it, Stacey would often add. But, alas, there was nothing to be seen that summer. The magic, it seemed, had all gone away. Had they grown too old, they wondered? Perhaps their help was no longer needed?

And now another summer had arrived, and they were beginning to doubt that they had ever seen the things they had seen or done the things they had done. The school year had been a hectic one, with lots and lots and lots of homework. And then there was the cornet to practice, and the Boy Scout badges to be earned, and the soccer games to be won. For Stacey, it was flute playing, choir singing, and ballet dancing. Busy, busy, busy, with little time for daydreams and no time for magic. And the busier they got, the longer their list of activities grew, the more they forgot the truth about themselves: that Alex was a hero and Stacey a princess. And all those wonderful words that had meant so much to them during their adventures—courage and honor and beauty and hope—lost their charm and their reality. As the gentle cooing of a morning dove is swallowed by the sound of rush hour traffic, so the thousand little details of their busy lives choked out the memories of all they had seen and done. The words became just that: words.

I hate to say it, but Alex and Stacey—they who had flown in the Chariot of the Sun and faced their deepest fears in the cave of the Cyclops—were beginning to lose sight of that which is most important and lasting. They were, in fact, becoming … well … adults.

Chapter

3

The Sounds of Battle

Alex and Stacey were supposed to be listening to the tour guide as he spoke passionately to a group of tourists about the last tragic days of the Alamo. But since the two children already knew all the details—Daddy was a better storyteller than any old tour guide—they quickly grew restless. To be honest, there was only one thing that they really wanted to do, only one thing that any true, red-blooded kid wants to do: explore! And I must say that the Alamo is a great place for exploring. Stony paths run off in every direction, leading you now to open, grassy spaces, now to secluded spots hidden along the corners of the wall. Only a few feet away, on the other side of the wall, the modern noises of San Antonio rushed by, but that only made it all the more strange. It was like discovering your own secret garden right in the middle of a bustling city. As for Alex and Stacey, their favorite parts were the long covered walkways and the maze of connected rooms that had been built right into the wall.

"Alex," said Stacey, when they had broken away from the group and were strolling along one of the walkways, "Do you think Davy Crockett stood on the same path we're on now?"

"I'm sure of it, Stacey," said Alex, "His spirit is all over this place. Didn't you feel it when we first walked through the chapel? And when we saw all those flags representing the states that Davy and the others came from? I wouldn't be surprised if this whole place were haunted."

"Alex," said Stacey, in a whisper so low he could barely hear her, "Do you think we could go back … back to the battle … just like we went back to Troy?"

"Oh, Stacey, let's not think about that again. There are no dreaming stones here, and I can't imagine Pan will be popping out of the wall anytime soon. Let's just forget about it."

"No!" insisted Stacey, "I won't forget about it! It was me who found the dreaming stone three years ago, and it will be me who will find something else today." And with that Stacey ran off toward one of the doors that led into the maze of rooms.

"Oh, brother," said Alex, "here she goes again." He had half a mind to leave her behind and return to the tour group and to his parents, but he still loved that crazy sister of his and worried about her quite a bit. So he did the only thing he could do: he ran off after her.

The Sounds of Battle

✦ ✦ ✦

Ten minutes later, having chased his sister through every room of the Alamo, Alex finally found her sitting on the grass with her head cradled in her hands. He could tell she was upset, and so he didn't tease her or even ask her what she was crying about. Instead, he took her hand gently and told her that if it would help, he would do some searching too. "After all," he said, "Daddy never did answer my question about freedom. I'll bet if I could ask Davy my question, he'd have a great answer. Alright, c'mon, we'll look together—you take that side of the wall and I'll take this side. Make sure you search every inch of it; you never know what might be hiding between the stones."

Stacey stopped crying immediately and began running her hands up and down the wall. Alex did the same, and for several minutes neither child said a word. They barely breathed. You see, they were concentrating very hard. Then, at the same exact moment, they both shouted: "Hey, what's this?"

One minute they had each been staring at a blank wall. The next minute there they were—two coonskin hats hanging like stockings from two rusty nails driven into the wall. As quickly as you can say, "remember the Alamo," Alex and Stacey swept the hats off of the nails and placed them firmly on their heads. Then Alex ran over to Stacey and gave her such a big hug that it lifted her right off of the ground.

"I can't believe it, Stacey," he shouted, "You were right. Maybe there *is* some magic left after all. But what do we do now?"

"I think we should spin, Alex. Remember two years ago when we found Pan hiding in my bedroom closet? He told us that he had traveled back in time by spinning so fast and hard that his tail grew and wrapped itself around him. I'll bet if we hold hands and spin together like we used to do when we played "ring around the rosy" that something magical will happen."

"No way, Stacey," said Alex, "You know that I hate spinning rides."

"No, Alex, it will be OK. You just have to believe."

Alex didn't like the idea at all, but Stacey insisted so hard that he finally gave in. Taking her right hand in his left and her left hand in his right, he began shuffling his feet to the right.

"Faster, Alex," said Stacey, "Faster!" With a sigh, Alex began to move his feet quicker and quicker. Stacey too picked up her pace and soon the two of them were whipping around like one of those spinning gates that you find in old playgrounds.

"Whee!" shouted Stacey, "This is more fun than ballet class."

And still they spun faster. And as they did, the two tails on their coonskin hats lifted higher and higher until they were pointing straight out behind their heads. As if they were living things, the tails began to hum loudly in the breeze, making a sound like a thousand crickets on a warm summer evening. And as they hummed, they began to glow: a deep green glow that radiated out from the ends of the tails and circled itself around the spinning children.

Soon, Alex and Stacey were moving so fast that if anyone had tried looking at them, he would have seen only a blur. Think of the four blades of a ceiling fan. When the fan is moving slowly, you can see each of the blades distinctly, but when the fan shifts into high speed, it soon becomes impossible to distinguish one blade from the other. In the same way, as the children's speed increased, it became more and more difficult to tell where Alex left off and Stacey began.

The Sounds of Battle

And still they spun faster, until all you could see was the green glow growing brighter and brighter. Locked inside that whirling green tornado, Alex and Stacey closed their eyes as tightly as they could and prayed that they wouldn't faint. The humming from the tails had grown so loud that it blocked out every other sound; it was like being locked up in the engine of a jet.

Then, just when the humming become so loud that Alex and Stacey were sure they would go deaf, a loud explosion cut through the air. Immediately, the humming stopped, the green glow disappeared, and Alex and Stacey were flung down to the ground.

"What was that explosion, Alex?" asked Stacey, after her head had stopped spinning.

"I'm not sure, Stacey," said Alex, as he blinked his eyes several times and rubbed the back of his neck, "It sort of sounded like fireworks."

Instantly, the explosion sounded again, and the children were left with no doubts as to what had caused it. It was a cannon!

Sensing the danger, the two children leaped to their feet and began looking wildly around them. They were in the middle of a battle. Men with rifles in their hands and knives in their belts were running in every direction. Everywhere there was shouting and screaming, and everywhere the noise of cannons and gunfire echoed in the still air. Alex and Stacey could tell by the sky that it was very early in the morning. The men around them looked tired and disheveled, as if they had all been aroused suddenly out of a very deep sleep.

Alex and Stacey were afraid they would be run over in all the madness, but nobody came near them or even seemed to notice them. Slowly, cautiously, they began to walk toward the wall. As they did, they studied more closely their surroundings. To their amazement, they discovered that the walls of the Alamo had grown; they now stretched around them in a huge circle. All along the wall, as far as the eye could see, they saw a series of low roofs and men lying on the roofs with their rifles propped up on the edge of the wall. When you looked at the faces of those men, you could tell they were afraid, and yet there was also a calm about them. They seemed to know in their hearts that they were in the right place at the right time, that this, somehow, was their destiny.

And then they saw *him*! There he was, less than ten feet away, with his coonskin hat on his head and his rifle clutched tightly in his hand. He was leaping from roof to roof, shouting orders to his men and firing his rifle at the oncoming soldiers. As they got closer to the wall, Alex and Stacey could see that the invading soldiers were carrying makeshift ladders over their heads. Dodging bullets and stones, each would lean his ladder up against the wall; when the ladders were secure, two or three other soldiers would scramble up each of them as fast as they could. Their plan, of course, was to leap over the wall and get inside the courtyard of the Alamo. But Davy Crockett wasn't about to let *that* happen. Each time the head of a Mexican soldier appeared above the wall, Davy would hit him with the butt of his rifle, sending him and the ladder flying back to the ground. He was a whirlwind of energy. At one point, Alex and Stacey watched in awe as Davy—in the space of only five seconds—shot one climbing soldier with his rifle, then turned it around and hit a second with the butt, and then kicked a third with the bottom of his right foot. One, two, three, the soldiers and their ladders crashed into the dirt. It was an amazing sight, so amazing that the children almost forgot to breathe.

The Sounds of Battle

After thirty minutes of heavy fighting, there was a brief lull in the battle, and Davy sat down to catch his breath. Immediately, Alex ran over to him and put out his right hand.

"Mr. Crockett," he said, "that was the finest shooting I've ever seen."

But Davy didn't shake his hand or even answer him back. In fact, he looked right through Alex as if he weren't there.

"That's not fair!" shouted Alex, clenching his fists with anger and frustration, "We come all the way back in time to the battle of the Alamo, and I can't even talk to Davy Crockett. Why should we be brought back here, if we can't talk with anyone?"

"Why don't we try shouting together, Alex?" said Stacey.

Alex nodded his head in agreement, and the two children began yelling out Davy's name on the top of their lungs. Anyone who had heard them would have had a headache for the next hour, but the yelling made no impression at all on Davy Crockett.

"Save your strength, children," said a voice behind them, "Davy cannot hear you. None of them can hear or see you. You are but two invisible onlookers here."

The sound of the voice startled Alex and Stacey, and they immediately swung around. Behind them stood the largest and strongest man they had ever seen. His legs were like massive tree trunks whose roots run deep into the earth; upon them rose a belly and chest that, to the children at least, appeared wider and thicker than the walls of the Alamo. His right hand was extended in greeting, while his left, as solid and powerful as the mast of a ship, clutched tightly a gnarled club. At first, the children thought that he was wearing a coonskin hat like Davy and a dark cloak, but when they looked more closely, they realized that the furry thing on his head was the face and mane of a lion and that what they thought was a cape was, in fact, the lion's shaggy hide. Though he was the one hero that Alex and Stacey had not met on their two journeys to ancient Greece, Alex knew at once who he was.

He was Hercules.

Chapter

4

The First Alamo

A lex had one annoying habit that drove his parents crazy. Whenever he was upset or shocked or just felt in the mood, he would take his right hand, ball it up into a tight fist, and smack it with great force against his forehead. He said it didn't hurt, but his parents were convinced he would someday give himself brain damage. Well, when Alex realized who it was who was standing in front of him, he hit his forehead so hard that even Stacey was afraid he would knock himself out. But the shock of seeing Hercules was so sudden and so strong that one smack was not enough for Alex. Two, three, four times he hit his forehead with his fist.

"My, oh my, young man," said Hercules, "with a lesser blow than that I knocked out the brains of the monster Geryon (GAIR yun) and defeated Cerberus (SIR bir us), the three-headed dog of Hades. You will need such strength if you are to accomplish the goal that has been assigned to you and your sister."

"Please, sir," said Stacey, who had not yet realized that the man in front of her was the greatest hero of ancient Greece and the strongest man who ever lived, "can you tell us why it is that no one here can see us but you? Are we or aren't we at the battle of the Alamo?"

"That, my dear," said Hercules, "is not an easy question to answer. You *are* here; there is no doubt about that. But you are also not here. Or rather, this place is not the endpoint of your journey; it's only a bouncing off place."

"A bouncing off place?" asked Alex, who had by now regained his composure and had stopped pounding on his forehead.

"Yes," said Hercules. "You see, although the gods granted me immortality and invited me to live with them on Mount Olympus, I do not possess as much magic as Pan, who came to you once before when the civilization of Greece and of all the world was in danger. I could not propel myself directly back to your time. I needed to find an in-between place where we could meet, a place that was linked both to my time and to yours."

"But, Hercules," said Alex, "I don't understand. How can your time and ours be linked by the Alamo?"

"Well," said Hercules, "it is easy to see how the Alamo is linked to you and your sister. You two are Texans, and the battle of the Alamo was the very crucible out of which Texas was born.

The First Alamo

But how it is linked to *my* time—well, if you can understand that, you will also understand why I have come all this way to meet you. You two are well known on Mount Olympus. My good friend, Theseus, told me the story of how you, Stacey, turned away the Minotaur with your mighty scream and how you, Alex, roped the beast's horn with your lasso. Thetis, she who is beloved by all the gods, told me all that you did for her poor son, Achilles, and Athena, daughter of Zeus, sang for me the tale of how you helped lead her favorite mortal, Odysseus, back home. I know too how you defeated the Accuser and set the course of civilization back on track.

"Children, you are needed again. Greece teeters on the edge of destruction. A rich and powerful tyrant—a tyrant beside whom this Santa Anna is but a mouse—threatens to crush all Greece and to steal from her her most precious treasure: freedom. Even now they have seized control of northern Greece and are marching southward. If they are not stopped, they will sweep down through all of Greece, and that continent you call Europe will be strangled in her crib—as I almost was by a terrible serpent. But before the invaders can conquer Greece, they must make their way through a narrow pass. With the sea on one side and mountains on the other, the only route into central Greece lies along this pass. If there is anywhere that the tyrant's army can be held back, it is here at a place we call Thermopylae (ther MA poe lee)—the "hot gates." And the army *must* be held back, at least for a short time.

"Greece is not a single nation; she is made up of a collection of small city-states that spend most of their time fighting against each other. The two strongest city-states are Athens, which lies in the center of Greece, and Sparta, which lies in the southern peninsula of Greece, what we call the Peloponnese. After much debate, the city-states have slowly begun to work together, but their army and navy are still not ready to meet the enemy. They need time to prepare, to organize, to regroup, and that time can only be bought for them by men willing to hold the pass of Thermopylae no matter the cost."

"Just like the Alamo!" said Alex and Stacey together.

"Yes, yes," said Hercules, "You are beginning to understand. Courage and heroism are things that rise above time and call out to each other across the vast spaces of history. Those who have taken their stand here at the Alamo are the brothers of those who stood two-thousand years earlier at the pass of Thermopylae. Both were willing to purchase freedom with their blood; both were willing to fight in a losing battle so that their side could win the war. At Thermopylae, as at the Alamo, every soldier will die, but they will inspire …"

"Alex," shouted Stacey, cutting off Hercules before he could finish his thought, "don't look now, but the three of us are floating off of the ground." And sure enough, Alex, Stacey, and Hercules were quickly rising upward; in no time at all, they found themselves hovering on a pocket of air a thousand feet above the battlefield.

"Don't be afraid," said Hercules, "It is the valor of these defenders of the Alamo that is causing us to rise, and it is that same valor that will fling us backward in time to Thermopylae."

Alex gritted his teeth, afraid that he and Stacey would start spinning again, but this time, rather than they being the ones to spin, it was the earth beneath them that began revolving faster and faster on its axis. Soon everything was a blur, and the children closed their eyes so that the sight would not make them dizzy.

The First Alamo

When they opened them again, several minutes later, they found that the Alamo and San Antonio had disappeared. Instead, they found themselves looking down on two things that one rarely sees when driving from Houston to San Antonio: mountains and the sea!

"Look!" said Hercules, pointing north with his finger, "Do you see the army marching southward?"

"Yes," said Alex, "I see it. I thought it was a river at first. I've never seen such a long line of people before. There must be hundreds of thousands of them. They stretch on for miles. How could anyone hold back an army like that?"

"And look now to the east where the sea rubs her back against the high cliffs. Do you see what is coming?"

"I see it," said Stacey, "It's a line of ships; they seem to go on forever. Are these ships too owned by the tyrant?"

"They are," said Hercules. "The tyrant's name is Xerxes (ZER xsees), and what you see stretched out before you are the armies and navies of Persia and her subject states. In less than twenty-four hours, they will reach the pass and will kill anyone who stands in their way. To stop such a force would be impossible, and yet the Greeks will do it. They will send Xerxes and his Persians running back to the East and, by so doing, will usher in the Golden Age of Greece. And out of that Golden Age, your civilization will be born. But this will only happen if the defenders of Thermopylae hold their ground as bravely and as truly as Davy Crockett. Look straight below you, and you will see them preparing for battle."

"But there are so few of them," cried Alex, "They couldn't possibly hold back the army that is coming. As far as I can see there are only a few hundred of them."

"Three hundred to be exact," said Hercules, "and all from the city of Sparta—home of the greatest soldiers in all Greece. If you look carefully, you will see several hundred more soldiers scattered along the pass who have come from Thebes and other city-states to help the Spartans. But when the end comes, it will be the three hundred who will stand alone. To be honest, the Spartan elders did not want to send even these three hundred; most of them saw no point in risking Spartan lives to defend a pass so far away from their city. But one of the two kings of Sparta saw it differently. He alone of all the Spartans understood that for Greece to be free, all Greeks, whatever their city-state, must stand together against their common foe. The three-hundred Spartans you see below you are his personal guard, hand-chosen by him for their courage and strength. He is a brave and noble general, and his name means the 'son of a lion.' He, children, is Leonidas (lay ON i das)."

"You say his name," said Stacey, "as if you knew him personally."

"I should," answered Hercules, "he is my great, great, great, great-grandson!"

Chapter
5

A Crisis of Faith

"Leonidas!" shouted Alex, "I've heard that name before, except that our Greek relatives pronounce it lay oh NEE thas. It was the name of my great-grandfather, my father's grandfather, I mean. And he was a Spartan. In fact, three summers ago, we visited Sparta, and saw the house where he was born."

"Yes," said Hercules, "I knew him well. It was I who breathed the courage into him to leave Greece and sail to America. And I know something else about him, something that no one in your family knows. Your great-grandfather, my young warrior, was a direct descendant of the Leonidas you see standing below you at the pass of Thermopylae. And that means, children, that you too are his descendants."

"But, Hercules," said Alex, taking a deep breath and opening his eyes as wide as he could, "that means that we must be *your* descendants too!"

"Exactly!" said Hercules, with a look of pride in his eyes, "why do you think you have been allowed three times now to journey backward to ancient Greece? Why do you think your father loves so much the old tales and has worked so hard to keep them alive in you? In each of you children, as in your father, there is a drop of my blood; it burns deep within you with the fire of all that is most noble. Yes, Alex, what you had always hoped was true *is* true—you *are* a hero and your sister *is* a princess. It is your true birthright!"

"Hercules," said Alex, throwing out his chest and lifting high his head, "We are ready to fulfill our mission. Give us each a sword, and we will fight alongside these three-hundred Spartans and alongside their leader, our ancestor."

"Your courage is great indeed," said Hercules, "Truly you are my descendants. But you do not understand. You have not been brought back here to fight. Brave though you are, there is little you could do on the battlefield to help the Spartans. No, you have been brought here for a much greater purpose.

"Your ancestor, as you rightly call him, has lost something far more important than strength of arms. He has lost his faith. Even now he looks out across the pass and wonders if it is all worth it. He is too wise a general to think that any of his men will survive the battle to come. Besides, before he left Sparta, he had heard a prophecy from the Oracle of Delphi that said if Greece was to survive the war, a King of Sparta must die. In his heart, he

A Crisis of Faith

knows that he is that King, and that it is his destiny to lay down his life for Sparta and for Greece. But he is troubled. When he left Sparta a week ago and headed for Thermopylae, he was quite sure that no price was too great to pay for the prize of freedom. Alas, that certainty has left him.

"You might as well know the truth now, children: Sparta is a hard and cruel place, more like an army barracks than a city. Oh, they are brave enough and will fight to the death to preserve their own freedom, but few of them understand what freedom—*true* freedom—really is. It is the Athenians, and the Athenians alone, who know what freedom means, who have lived it out in their assemblies, in their courts, in their lives. Leonidas knows this, and that is why he is here: why he refused to remain behind in Sparta; why he insisted on working together with the Athenians for the good of all Greece."

"Hercules," said Alex, "I still don't understand what you want us to do."

"Alex," said Hercules, with sadness in his voice, "Leonidas has forgotten why he is here. He has forgotten what freedom means, has come to doubt that it is anything more than a word. You must teach him what it means. If you do not do this, if you cannot convince him that freedom is real and precious enough to die for, then I fear that when the morning comes, my royal descendant—and with him, his men—will abandon his post. And if that happens, the armies of Xerxes will ravage the land of Greece and turn her, as she has already turned most of Asia, into a subject state. All of Greece will be enslaved to Persia, and the history of the West will be changed forever. The pass below you is the crux, the crossroads where all the paths converge.

"But come, let us descend to the tent of Leonidas that you may teach him the true nature of freedom and the reason why it must be defended. Alex, you are the eldest; you must be the one who speaks to him."

For one long minute, no one said anything. Stacey looked down at her feet, while Alex turned his gaze away from the searing, hopeful eyes of Hercules. With each passing second, Alex's face grew redder and redder, and his mouth grew dryer and dryer. He had the look of one who has been trapped and searches desperately for a way of escape.

"But, Hercules," he finally managed to say, "I … I … I can't … I can't do this thing … I don't know …" His voice trailed away, and he covered his face with his hands. Stacey, who knew well her brother's moods, could tell that he was crying but that he didn't want Hercules to know that he was. By now, Stacey had gotten pretty good at floating in the air and so it only took her a second to position herself between Alex and Hercules.

"Please, Hercules," she said, "You can't ask my brother to do this. He doesn't know what freedom is any more than I do or Leonidas does. We are just children. What do we know about freedom? Earlier today, Alex even asked Daddy to explain to us why freedom was so important, but he never got the chance to answer Alex's question. Please, ask him to do something else. My brother is smart and brave. There must be some other way to help those Spartans down there."

"I was afraid this might happen," said Hercules, "Zeus warned me that freedom was a thing that children had but did not understand, and that adults understood but did not have. I fear, children, that your world, like Leonidas, has forgotten its heritage of freedom—has perhaps taken it for granted. But do not despair.

A Crisis of Faith

There is another way. It is longer and more fraught with danger, but I think it can be done. You have come back thus far in time; now you must go further back into the dim beginnings of Athens, the mother of freedom.

"Yes, for a brief moment, you must return to the world of myth. Once there, a second guide will direct you forward, back into the flow of history. You must see firsthand all the strands that have led to this point. You must see how Athens first became a democracy, how she learned to value freedom and to build it into the life of her city. When you have done this, when you have seen for yourselves the foundations of freedom, I shall return to you and take you away to Persia. If you are to understand freedom fully, then you must understand as well its opposite. You must see the opposing forces, the opposing ideas that led to this terrible conflict between East and West, tyranny and freedom. Only then, when you have gained a full perspective, will you be ready to explain to Leonidas why he must hold the pass no matter the cost to himself and his men."

"Hercules," said Alex, who had stopped crying and was eager again to fulfill his mission, "we are ready to do as you ask. Send us back. We are not afraid."

"Yes!" said Hercules with a voice as deep as the sea. Then, "Good!" with a voice as powerful as the thunder. And then, with the force of a hurricane, "GO!" As he said the third word, Hercules threw out his hands in the direction of Alex and Stacey. The movement of his hands stirred up a mighty wind that blew the children backward. Head over heels they rolled, like tumbleweeds caught in a storm. No Olympic gymnast has ever flipped so fast and so far as Alex and Stacey did in that exhilarating, terrifying moment.

For the first three flips they laughed; for the second three they screamed; by the seventh, they were both unconscious.

Chapter 6

The Trial

Stacey, who never got dizzy no matter how many times she spun around, was the first to regain consciousness. To her surprise, she found that she was lying next to her brother on the side of a gently sloping hill that was dotted all over with the cutest goats and sheep she had ever seen. Her first instinct was to run over and pet them, but she thought she had better wake up Alex first. And so, standing up and shaking the dust off of her clothes, she let one enormous yawn escape from her mouth and then bent down toward her sleeping brother. Her plan was to grab Alex's shoulder and give it a good firm shake, but before she could do so, someone else grabbed *her* shoulder and gave *it* a good shake.

"Oh," screamed Stacey, and whirled around as fast as she could. Living with an older brother had made her into quite a good wrestler, and before the stranger knew what was happening, Stacey had knocked him to the ground and was sitting on his chest.

"Who are you?" she said, "and what do you want?"

"Please, fair nymph," said the young man, who looked to Stacey to be about the age of one of Daddy's college students, "I mean you no harm. On the contrary, I need your help. I am being pursued by the most hideous creatures in all of Greece. They have snakes for hair and poison drips from their fangs. Please, if you know a place I can hide, tell me where it is."

"Who are these creatures?" said Stacey, "They sound like Gorgons to me, and I *hate* Gorgons. Once before I helped Perseus to kill Medusa, and I even cut one of the snakes off her sister's ugly head. I'm not afraid of Gorgons!"

"You are a brave young woman indeed," said the stranger, "but these beasts who pursue me are not Gorgons, but Furies. Like the Gorgons, they are born of the earth and of night, and like them as well, they are tireless in their evil. The Furies are the bloodhounds of Hades; they chase down all those who have committed a terrible crime against their family."

"A terrible crime?" said Stacey, "What is it you have done?"

"I will not lie to you, O nymph of Athens. I have killed my own mother."

"Get away from me," said Stacey, "Why should I help a man who has done something like that?"

The Trial

"But I had no choice! My mother killed my father, and the god Apollo chose me to avenge my father's death. I am trapped … I cannot escape this torment … I …"

With a wild convulsion, the stranger was thrown to the ground and began rolling madly in the dirt. He flailed his hands at the empty air around him as though he were fighting an invisible enemy. On his face, there was a look of pain that twisted and contorted all of his features. It was all so horrible that Stacey hugged her arms to her chest and began to scream.

"It's alright, Stacey," said a voice behind her that made her spin around almost as fast as the stranger had, "I know who he is. His name is Orestes (oh RESS tees), and he is the son of Agamemnon (a ga MEM non). Don't you remember the story, Stacey? In order to get the Greek fleet safely to Troy, Agamemnon agreed to sacrifice his own daughter. When he returned home ten years later, his wife, Clytemnestra (cly tim NESS tra), lured him into a bathtub and stabbed him to death. Seven years after that, Orestes, who had been in hiding with a relative, returned to the palace of Agamemnon, where, with the help of his sister, Electra, he killed his mother."

"Now I remember the story, Alex, but why is he being chased by the Furies?"

"I guess because there is no one left in his family to avenge his mother's death. If I remember the story right, Apollo told Orestes that the only hope he had of escaping the vengeance of the Furies was to flee to Athens and seek the help of Athena."

"Athena!" said Stacey, "If that's why he's come here, then maybe we *can* help him. Three years ago, after we helped Perseus to cut off Medusa's head, we brought the head here to Athens and gave it to Athena to put on her shield. Do you remember, Alex?"

"Yes, of course I do, Stacey, but do you think that Athena will remember us?"

"We goddesses do not forget such deeds easily. The head of Medusa still rests in the center of my shield, and it has frightened away many an enemy."

For the third time in the last five minutes, Stacey spun around to find standing behind her a tall, stately woman in a flowing gown. In her right hand, she held a spear, and perched on her shoulder was a very sleepy-looking owl. Both children recognized her at once. She was Athena.

"Goddess," said Alex, in his most adult voice, "We have been sent here by Hercules to learn the true nature of freedom that we might in turn explain it to Leonidas the Spartan. But before we can do that, we beg of you to help this young man. He has been sent here by Apollo to seek your guidance and protection. Please, Athena, you cannot leave him to the mercy of those horrible Furies. They don't care about justice; all they seek is revenge."

"Well spoken, young Odysseus (oh DISS ee us)," said Athena, "Your travels with the noble father of Telemachus (te LE ma kus) have taught you well the art of speaking persuasive words. I will help *both* you and the unfortunate Orestes. Indeed, you have already pointed the way with your wise words. Justice is exactly what I intend to seek for the son of Agamemnon, but this same justice lies at the very heart of that freedom you seek.

"I mean to establish this very day the first court of justice in the world. True, for many centuries the elders of villages have decided the disputes that were brought before them, but today I shall lay the foundations for a more permanent court that shall rise above all slander, all envy, all favoritism. I shall make the Law a thing that no man can bend to his own designs. Apart from such a Law, there can be no true freedom. Let that be your first lesson, children. Freedom does not mean the power to do anything you want, but the power to do that which is right.

"But come now, let us ascend the hill of the Acropolis, where I shall assemble the twelve wise men who shall make up my court. All must be ready when the Furies arrive."

✦ ✦ ✦

The next few hours were a flurry of activity. Orestes had regained his sanity and was now sitting calmly on a large stone in the center of the Acropolis. In front and slightly above him, there stretched a long, slightly curved table that Athena had carved out of a single slab of marble. Behind the desk, twelve chairs, also made of marble, were placed side by side, and upon those chairs, sat twelve men with white beards and dark brown eyes. At the center, with six men to the right of her and six to the left, stood Athena herself, resplendent in her pure white robe.

"Judges of Athens," she said, "You have been chosen both for your wisdom and for your fairness. In your hands rests the fate of Orestes. Indeed, not only his fate, but the fate of all who come after him, lies now before you. Let not yourselves be swayed by fancy words or expensive bribes or ugly threats. What you do and decide this day shall be like a stone thrown into the pond; your words and your deeds shall ripple outwards in ever widening circles until all of Athens, all of Greece, all the world shall feel their force. What we do here today shall be a thing for all time. It is my will, and that of my father Zeus and of my brother Apollo, that this land shall be civilized by the twin powers of Justice and Law. But we cannot do this thing alone. You must do your part. You must move beyond your own fears and prejudices to embrace those higher truths that come only from above. Are you ready to take on this task?"

"We are," said the twelve together, and as they did, the Acropolis shook beneath them.

"It is well," said Athena, "but now, look sharp! The accusers of Orestes have entered your court."

When Athena spoke these words, Alex and Stacey turned at once and looked behind them. What they saw would stay in their minds forever. Three hideous women were leaping towards them in great pouncing strides. Where their noses and mouths should have been, they had beaks like those of vultures, and from those beaks, a stream of black poison dripped steadily to the ground. Their hair was a mass of snakes that swayed back and forth in the wind, now biting at each other, now biting at their owner. At first, the children thought they were dressed in red robes, but as they drew closer, Alex and Stacey saw, to their horror, that what they really wore were torn rags soaked in human blood. Around their waists were leather belts, and from their belts hung the skulls of a dozen men.

"We have come for Orestes," they cried out in unison, their voices more like the croaking of frogs than the shouts of women, "His life and his blood belong to us. Surrender him now."

"I shall not," said Athena, boldly, "This man is under the protection of Apollo, the very god who called upon him to kill the murderer of his father. Apollo shall speak on his behalf."

"Where is Apollo?" the Furies cried, "We do not see him. This murderer has no one to speak for him."

"Apollo will come," said Athena, "He must have been delayed."

The Trial

"He will never come," said the Furies, "Orestes is ours, and we shall take him—unless, of course, there is someone else here who will speak on his behalf."

"I shall speak," said Alex, and strode forward toward the table. "I too know the laws of Zeus, and I know that there is nothing more sacred in the eyes of heaven than the guest and the suppliant. Zeus is the god of guests, and he demands that hospitality and sanctuary be given to all who are strangers in the land. Once before, on my journeys with Odysseus, I met a monster like you. He was a Cyclops, and his name was Polyphemus (pa lee FEE mus). He dared to violate the guest-host relationship and devour the men of Odysseus. His punishment was swift; the noble Odysseus put out his one great eye with a spear. So speak no more of taking away this boy; he is our suppliant and as such is sacred to Zeus. It is these judges, not you, who shall decide his fate!"

"That's telling them," said Stacey, "You go, Alex!"

Alex was tempted to wave back at Stacey, but he thought that would be too informal and make him look like a kid. So he only turned his head slightly and winked at her with his right eye. To be honest, he was scared to death, but he wasn't going to let the Furies know it.

"So," said the Furies, "you dare to call on Zeus to cover the crimes of this murderer. You shall not rob us of our rightful prey. *We* are the accusers, and he is the accused."

"Not so fast, you snake-heads," said Alex, "I happen to know a thing or two about accusers. It was *I* who helped to save Achilles from the lies of the Accuser when he tempted the Greek warrior to kill the father of the dead Hector. Yes, and it was I too—I and my sister—who helped to break the hold of the Accuser when he tempted Odysseus and Telemachus to kill the families of the evil suitors who had defiled his home with their greed and folly. You, then, will be no more than he was.

"You do not seek justice or life or truth; you seek only revenge and death and despair. What good will it do to kill this boy? There has been enough blood and betrayal in his family. He was chosen by Apollo to put an end to the cycle of revenge, but you would keep that cycle going on and on forever. You know yourselves that Orestes has been to the Oracle of Delphi and has purified himself of all guilt."

"Guilt like his cannot be purified," shrieked the Furies, "Blood calls out for blood. That is the way it has always been and ever shall be. Skin for skin is the only law we know."

"Yes," said Alex, "it is the only law that *you* know, but it is not the only law. There is a higher one, one that your world has yet to see, but it is coming."

"Alex," whispered Stacey, "tell them what we read in Sunday school last week. You know, the verse from Isay, Isee; oh, I can never pronounce his name."

"Do you mean Isaiah, Stacey?"

"Yes, Isaiah. It was from the first chapter, but I can't remember the verse."

Alex thought for a moment, and then his eyes flashed with fire: "Yes, Stacey, I *do* remember it now. Listen to me, you Furies, and hear the words of a prophet who is almost as ancient as yourselves: 'Come now, and let us reason together, saith the Lord: though your sins be as scarlet, they shall be as white as snow; though they be red like crimson, they shall be as wool.' Orestes has been purified by Apollo and the Oracle. Red has given way to white."

"Stop," cried the Furies, "your words burn in our ears. This boy is guilty, and he must pay the penalty. We will no longer listen to your speeches. We call on the judges to render their verdict now."

"Very well" said Athena, "let the judges now decide the fate of Orestes."

No sooner were her words spoken than Alex, Stacey, Orestes, and the Furies fell silent. As the judges spoke quietly together, it seemed to the children that the very sun stood still in the heavens. After what seemed many hours, the oldest of the judges stood and faced Orestes:

"We have reached our verdict, Orestes. Six of us find you innocent; the other six find you guilty." And then, turning to Athena: "Goddess, you must cast the deciding vote."

"I say the boy is innocent; his guilt is no longer to be held against him. Orestes, son of Agamemnon, you are free to return to your land and to do what you can to restore order and peace. In you rests the future; do not squander the gift that has been given you."

"No," shrieked the Furies in unison, "we shall not be treated like this. We renounce our claim on Orestes' blood, but in return we shall ravage the land of Athens. We shall cause your crops to wither and your cattle to sicken and die. We shall bring drought and famine and plague. You shall see that we are not goddesses to be trifled with."

"Move one step closer, spawn of Hades," yelled Athena, "and I shall kill you where you stand. Speak again your curses and I shall call on my father Zeus to strike you with his deadly thunderbolt."

"Wait!" shouted Stacey, and ran into the space between the Furies and Athena, "You are both wrong. All my life I have hated

Gorgons, and when I first saw these Furies I thought only of cutting off their snakes with a sword. But now I think differently. If Orestes can be forgiven, then so too can the Furies. Please, Athena, let me speak to them, and promise me that you will do whatever I ask."

"You are a strange child," said Athena, "almost as strange as your brother. But you both seem to know of a wisdom that I, the goddess of wisdom, do not know. Proceed, child."

"Furies," said Stacey, "all your lives you have been hated and despised because you did a job that no one else wanted to do. What if Athena were to allow you to live here in Athens and to take on a new job: a job that would make you loved and honored by all the people. You tried to kill Orestes because he killed the mother that killed his father. If you hate so much those who destroy their families, then you must believe that families are special. Why not stay here then, and use your powers to bless marriage and to protect childbirth. I am sure if you said yes that Athena would build you a new home, perhaps a cave under this very Acropolis, where you could work goodness instead of evil."

"Your wisdom is indeed from the gods," said Athena, "Daughters of the night, if you agree, I will do the very thing this child asks. In a cave beneath this hill, you shall live and do your work. The marriage bed shall be yours to bless, and all my people shall love and worship you. Each year, they will bring flowers to your cave and sing hymns to your goodness and mercy. Come then, children of the earth, and let us reason together. Let the chaos and the anger and the vengeance end. Let civilization begin!"

"We agree, O Daughter of Zeus," said the Furies, "Since you honor us in this way, we will put aside our wrath and become a blessing to your city."

The Trial

And then, before the startled eyes of Alex and Stacey, a wondrous change came over the Furies. Their snakes stopped twisting and turned into strands of golden hair. Their beaks grew softer and were transformed into delicate noses and rounded lips. Their rags fell off, and they were clothed anew in robes of purest white. Athena raised her spear and tapped it once against the earth. Immediately, the ground behind her sank inward to form a marble stairway. Down the stairs the Furies, their hatred gone, descended in a flurry of white robes and golden hair.

"Well done, children," exclaimed Athena, "You have traveled all this way to learn of me, and instead I have learned of you. You have helped to lay the foundations of Athenian freedom. All has been set in motion, though it will take many centuries to unfold. Mortals, I am afraid, are very slow learners.

"But enough talk. Lay your hands upon my robe, and I shall take you forward in time. We must travel six-hundred years into the future, where you will meet the man who first turned the minds and hearts of Athens toward democracy and freedom. As we travel, I shall tell you how it all began."

Chapter 7

The Founding Father

Just as she had promised, Athena explained to Alex and Stacey that after the days of Orestes, Athens, like all Greece, fell into a dark age when the skills of reading and writing were lost, and men, forgetting the higher things, thought only of simple survival. For many farmers, life was rough; good land was hard to find, and the soil was so dry and rocky that it yielded few crops to those who broke their backs to till it. But things were different in Athens and in the larger region of which Athens was the capital.

In that region, which the Greeks called Attica, there was plenty of room, and to spare, and the soil was rich and well watered.

Eventually, the Greeks learned again to read and write—they even made themselves a new alphabet, different than the one used by the heroes of Troy—and they began to turn their thoughts back to more noble pursuits. In this they were helped by two great poems, newly composed by a blind poet named Homer, that sang of the timeless virtues of peace and war and of what happens when those virtues are lost.

At this point, Alex couldn't help but break in: "You mean the *Iliad* and the *Odyssey*! The reason we were brought back to ancient Greece two years ago was to help make sure those poems were written by making sure the Trojan War and the journeys of Odysseus happened in the right way."

"Yes, children," said Athena, "that is precisely the reason you were brought back. And soon you shall see just how important the *Iliad* and *Odyssey* were for my beloved Athenians. It was on the back of those wonderful tales that Athens, and through her, all Greece, built her civilization. But it took some time. At first, Attica thought little of the higher virtues. When the land is rich and crops are plenty, there is little need for assemblies or governments or culture. I'm afraid my people needed a stronger incentive to learn to work together for the greater good of all and to learn the fuller meaning of freedom. As long as things went well in Attica, freedom meant only minding your own business and ignoring everyone around you.

"All that changed when drought and famine struck the land of Attica. Poor farmers, to prevent their families from starving, sold first their land and then themselves to rich landlords who began to treat them like slaves. A great outcry rose up throughout

The Founding Father

Athens and all of Attica. At first, the situation looked grim. I feared my people would call in a powerful warlord to settle their problems for them. Oh children, how quick you mortals are to sell your freedom and your birthright to a tyrant if only he will promise you security and revenge against all those you would blame for your troubles. Beware: the tyrant always takes far more than he gives.

"Rulers there were aplenty who would have gladly seized control of Athens, but the Athenians chose the more difficult route. Yes, in the end, they *did* turn over all power and authority in Attica to a single ruler—they could think of no other solution—but the ruler they chose was neither a tyrant nor a warlord. They chose instead one of the seven sages of Greece, a man famous for his wisdom and insight: a scholar, a poet, a lover of Homer. His name, children, is Solon (SEW lon), and it is to his care I shall now turn you over. Watch him; learn from him. Perhaps you can even help him as you have helped me.

"It has now been two years since Greece celebrated her 45th Olympic games—594 BC by your calendar—and Solon has just been handed the reins of government. For the next hundred years, Athens will slowly grow and develop until she becomes the great mistress of freedom. You shall witness that growth with the help of my pet owl. Stacey, would you like to hold her."

"Oh yes, Athena," said Stacey, "I would love to!"

"Good," said Athena, "then stretch out your arm. As long as the owl remains with you, you will be safe from all harm. Pay careful attention to her. Each time she hoots and flaps her wings, you and your brother will leap forward in time. You will never know exactly how many years ahead you will be leaping, so keep focused and watch for clues. Often when you leap, you will meet the same people, but they will, of course, be older. Don't be fooled by appearances. Keep your eyes and ears opened."

"We will," said Alex.

"I knew I could trust you both," said Athena, "Truly does the blood of Hercules flow through your veins. There is more I would like to tell you, but behold, we have arrived. Alex, do you see that hut in front of you?"

"I do," said Alex.

"That," said Athena, "is the home of Solon. Though he is now the ruler of Athens, he has chosen to remain in his humble cottage. Stacey, be sure to take good care of my owl; she is my most precious treasure."

Stacey turned her head toward Athena, intending to thank her for entrusting her with her owl, but Athena was gone.

With slightly shaky legs, but a firm resolve, Alex and Stacey approached the hut alone.

❖ ❖ ❖

Athena had told the children that Solon was a lover of Homer, and if loving Homer meant loving the guest-host relationship, then Solon was a lover indeed. Before the children got within fifty feet of his hut, Solon ran out to greet them and invited them to share his supper. Being a good host, he asked them no questions until they had eaten their fill of food and were reclining comfortably before the fire. Even then, he did not question them at once, but took from a corner of his hut a six-stringed lyre and began to strum it softly. As he played, he sang:

Seven times ten are allotted a man for the length of his days.
First are the years of the infant, growing his two sets of teeth;

The Founding Father

Two sevens more follow fast on the first, turning youth into man.
Off to Olympia they ride, while the sun of the fourth
seven shines;
See them in all of their glorious beauty! Even the gods
Gaze from Olympus, staring in wonder at Man in his prime.
Next come the years when a man turns his thoughts to the
opposite sex,
Woe to him then if the size of his heart be no match for his arm!
These are the years of the husband and father—each day is
precious.
Then, in the midst of his seventy years, man changes his life:
Love for the body gives way in its turn to the love of the mind.
Reason is king in the sixth age; speech in the seventh and eighth.
Pray that they both will continue, all through the years of
the ninth.
He that shall live through the tenth without strife is beloved of
the gods.
These are the ages allotted to man—but heed my advice:
Some say that those in the fourth age are happiest; I disagree.
Count no man lucky until he has lived to the end of his days
Only if then he can look back with gladness and pride is he blest.
Such the uncertainty, such the distress of our seventy years.

"That was beautiful," said Stacey, when Solon had finished his song and put back his lyre, "It reminds me of the time when my brother and I sat in the tent of Achilles and heard him sing sadly a song about war."

"*Achilles*, you say," said Solon, "You must be quite a bit older than you look. I knew at once there was something mysterious about you two. I am not so old a fool that I did not recognize the owl of Athena on your arm. Never would I dare to harm one who is her favorite, for it is she of all the gods who most loves our city of Athens."

"Yes," said Alex, "that is true. Athena *does* love your city; it is she who has sent us. My name is Alex, and this is my sister, Stacey. Athena told us that you would teach us the true meaning of freedom and that perhaps we might help you to set things right in Athens."

"I accept," said Solon, "The Athenians have lain upon me a heavy burden, and I welcome help from any friends of Athena. I take it the goddess has explained to you the situation?"

"She has," answered Alex, "and now I suppose that you will set everyone free and make them all equal and let them all decide together what is to be done."

"Zeus forbid!" said Solon. "If I were to do such a thing, I would be inviting a catastrophe. Freedom can't simply be given away; it has to be earned and learned. Imagine what would happen if you set a feast before a starving man or a great treasure before a beggar. Neither man would know what to do with his gift: the first would gorge himself until he got sick; the second would quickly waste away all that he was given. In the end, you would have produced not virtue and freedom, but gluttony and greed. No man can use freedom properly until he has learned to wait patiently for the things he wants and to distinguish between his wants and his needs."

The Founding Father

As soon as Solon had spoken his last sentence, Alex looked at Stacey and Stacey looked at Alex, and they both blurted out together: "delayed gratification!"

"What's that you are saying, children?"

"Delayed gratification," said Alex, "It's something our father talks about all the time.

"Three or four times now he has sat us down together and told us that the secret to living a happy life is delayed gratification. It took us both a while to figure out what the words meant. Gratification means getting something you really want; delayed means waiting to get it. Daddy told us that most people—not just kids, but adults too!—insist on having things right away, and because of that they end up making very bad decisions and owing money to everybody."

"Your father is a wise man, children. Without temperance, without self-control, there can be no true freedom. Sometimes the only way you can have freedom in a city is by making laws that hold back greed the way a bridle holds back a horse."

"Alex," whispered Stacey, "tell him what Daddy told us about Moses and the Ten Commandments."

"What are you talking about, Stacey?"

"You know, Alex, about slaves becoming freemen, not freemen becoming slaves."

"Oh yes," said Alex, "that's a good idea!"

"What are you two whispering about?" said Solon.

"Solon," said Alex, "I don't know if you've heard about them, but there is another race of people who are much older than the Greeks, and who were lucky to have a man like you to teach and guide them. They are called the Jews or the Israelites, and they were called by God—not one of *your* gods, but the one true God who has always existed and who created the universe—to be his chosen people. For four-hundred years they were slaves in Egypt, until God sent a man named Moses to lead them out of slavery into a new land. On the way to that new land, God met Moses on a mountain and gave him a set of ten laws that all the people were to follow.

"When we first heard the story, we wondered why God would free them from slavery and then turn around and give them more rules to follow. But Daddy told us that God did not give those laws to a group of freemen to make them into slaves, but to a group of former slaves in order to make them freemen. He told us that without those Ten Commandments, and all the other smaller laws that came with them, the Jews would not have known how to behave, but would have gone crazy, like kids sometimes do when the teacher leaves the room. Without those laws, he said, they would have ended up getting themselves in such a mess that they would have had to chose a new tyrant to fix everything up."

"I have heard some rumors in the past of these people. I hope someday that I can meet them and learn more of their God and their laws. But tell me, Alex, did these Jews ever get into a situation like the one we have in Athens? Did any of them lose their lands and become slaves to their own fellow Israelites?"

"Of course," said Alex, "I'm glad you asked that question, Solon. When God spoke to Moses on the mountain, he ordered him to do something special every fifty years. The people were allowed to sell their land and even themselves to the richer landlords, but when the fiftieth year came, all debts would be cancelled, and the land would go back to its original owners. They called it the … the …"

"The Jubilee!" yelled Stacey, "It was called the Jubilee. I always liked that word."

"Truly you children have been sent by Athena," said Solon, "This very day I shall declare a Jubilee throughout all the lands of Attica. All debts will be forgiven, all slaves set free, but that is as far as I shall go. What belongs rightfully to the rich, they shall keep, and if the poor wish to keep their lands, then they must work hard to make them prosper. No one shall be allowed to steal from the poor and to take away their liberty, but neither shall the poor be allowed to steal from the rich."

"Then you *will* make everyone equal, after all," said Alex.

"No, Alex," said Solon, "I will not. Only slaves are all the same; freemen are unique. Yes, I will give everyone in Athens equal protection under the law, but the control of government I shall reserve for those who own land. If a poor man with no land is given power, he might easily become a tyrant: after all, he has nothing to lose if Athens prospers or falls. But the man who owns land in Attica will work hard to keep the government running smoothly and fairly. I shall divide the power between those who are rich and come from old families and those whose lands are smaller and whose blood is less noble. Each shall serve on a different council. Together they shall govern Attica."

"This year in school," said Stacey, "we learned that there are two groups who work together to make laws for our country: the Senate and the House. Every few years, all the adults vote on who they want to represent them. That's how our democracy works."

"Democracy," said Solon, "that's an interesting word. It means 'rule by the people.' Yes, I like it. We shall call our government a democracy as well. But I don't know if I like this idea of voting. If we did that, the rich people might try to get out of serving on the council. No, we shall not elect our council-members by vote, but select them by lot. This way, all of them will have to serve at some point, and all of them will learn that they have a stake in the future of Athens. They must learn that it means something to be a citizen of Athens. And to show them how special and precious that citizenship is, I shall open the doors of Attica and allow foreign craftsmen to come to our city and earn their citizenship. In our land, those who have power and land shall respect the law, for they will have had a hand in making it. As for the common people, they shall be given the chance to serve on the jury and vote on who is guilty or innocent. They too must learn that in Athens, the law is supreme."

"Yeah!" shouted Alex and Stacey together, "You've done it, Solon. You've found the solution."

With their arms stretched out, the children rushed over to Solon to give him a hug, but before they could reach him, the owl—which had now moved up to Stacey's shoulder—gave out a loud hoot and flapped its wings. Immediately, Solon and his cottage disappeared, and the children found themselves on a lonely road at the very edge of Attica.

Chapter 8

The Chosen

"What happened, Alex?" said Stacey, when her head had stopped spinning.

"I think Athena's owl just sent us forward in time. Look around and see if there is anybody else here but us. The place looks empty to me."

"I don't see anyone, Alex," said Stacey, as she strained her eyes in every direction, "We seem to be the only ones ... Wait! Over there in the distance. Someone is coming this way."

Both children stood motionless for the next few minutes as they tried to see who it was that was coming toward them. As the figure got closer, they could see it was an older man and that he was dressed for a long journey. He had a white beard and carried a cane."

"Ah, children," he said, when he was close enough to see their faces clearly, "I feared when you disappeared from my hut that I would never see you again! Praise be to Athena that she has sent you back to me."

"Solon," shouted Alex with glee, "is it really you? But why do you look so much older?"

"Many years have passed, my son, since we last met. They have been hard ones for me. These Athenians are so ungrateful. No matter what I do, they bicker and complain. Still, for all their complaining, I have managed to keep the peace and to stop them from enslaving themselves again. But I grow weary of the fight. I fear I gave them too much freedom. Maybe they weren't ready for it. I thought the greatest threat to my democracy would be an unwillingness to serve in the government. But I was wrong. The greatest danger is envy. The poor envy the middle class, the middle class envy the rich, and the rich envy each other. Needless to say, everybody envies me! Even now three different factions have sprung up in the hill country, along the shoreline, and on the grassy plains. Some want to give more power to the people; others want to take it away completely. The ones in the middle don't know what they want. I tell you, I'm sick of it. They must figure it out for themselves.

"As for me, I'm about to take a much-needed vacation. For the next ten years, I intend to travel through the countries of the East and study their cultures and their governments. Most of all, I want to meet those Jews that you told me about. I want to hear more of their God and of the law he gave them. Children, why don't you come with me? We could travel together."

"Would we?" said Alex, "Of course we would! When do we start?"

"Right now," said Solon, "I'm on my way to the sea where I shall rent a boat and sail for the Coast of Ionia."

"I love boats," said Stacey, "Our grandfather has a beautiful one ..."

But that's as far as she got. Before she could finish her sentence, the owl hooted again and flapped its wings, and everything around them went black.

✦ ✦ ✦

"I'm not sure that I like traveling through time, Alex," said Stacey, who, as always, was the first one to recover from their dizzying journeys, "Where do you think we are now?"

"We seem to be in the hills of Attica this time," said Alex, "I wonder if there's anybody here that we know ... Oh my gosh, there he is! It's Solon again."

And sure enough, there was Solon, still dressed in his traveling clothes and still carrying his cane. But this time he looked even older than before. Both children could see that he wasn't long for our world. Still, beneath the worry lines and the gray hair, they could still recognize the fire of wisdom in his eyes.

"So, my fellow travelers, we meet once more. It has been several years now since my return to Attica. I did so hope I would see you again."

"How was your journey, Solon?" asked Stacey, "Did you ever find the Jews?"

"I did indeed, child," said Solon, "and they have half convinced me to follow their God. I learned of their great king, David, and of the wisdom of his son, Solomon. But alas, children, I have sad news for you. Only eight years after I was chosen ruler of Athens, the kingdom of the Jews was ravaged by the cruel Babylonians. Their glorious temple was razed to the ground and their people taken into captivity. Beside my own fellow Greeks, they are the only people I have met in my travels who have any real understanding of freedom. Their law, children, is a thing of beauty, as is their sense of their own destiny. Even now, as they suffer in slavery to Babylon, they believe firmly in that destiny. I only pray that my Athenians, and through them the Greeks, will one day learn that they too have a destiny. But I fear that before that time comes, my dear Greeks will have to suffer.

"Children, while I was in Babylon, I met one of their priests, a man named Daniel. From him I learned a marvelous tale: the Jewish God, he said, rescued them from the Egyptian army by splitting a sea in half and letting them walk through the midst of it as though on dry ground. And when the Egyptians pursued them in their chariots, their leader, Moses, raised his staff, and the waters closed upon the Egyptians. It was at that moment, the priest told me, that his people knew beyond any doubt that they were chosen to do wondrous things. They were to be a special people set apart by God to be a blessing to all the nations. Indeed, through the line of David, there would one day come, so believed Daniel, a Messiah to save them. I have never met a man so at peace as this Daniel. With prophetic words, he told me that in the years ahead three great kingdoms would follow Babylon, each more mighty than the one before it, but that during the time of the last, the Messiah would be born and set the foundations for a new kingdom that would never end. Ah, children, if only I could live to see that day!

"But now I must think of Greece. As I see my death approach, it becomes clearer and clearer to me that Greece will only find her true destiny when her back is pushed against the wall, and she sees the enemy close around her. If then, at that moment, when all is lost, the sea parts and Greece is saved—then, and only then, will she become the nation she was born to be."

"All of these things will happen, Solon, just as you say," said Alex, "This I can promise you. We have been brought back in time to make sure that they happen."

"Good, good," said Solon, "you have restored my faith. Since my return several years ago, I've studied the situation in Athens, and it has filled me with great fear. As I told you before leaving on my journey, Attica is broken into three factions. For awhile, the three groups were equal in their power, but then, a new leader rose up among the people of the hill country. His name was Peisistratus (pie ZIS tra tus), and he was as smart as he was strong. By a ruse worthy of Odysseus himself, Peisistratus went into the hills and cut himself all over with a knife. Then, he returned to the city and told the council that he had been attacked by enemies. Playing on their sympathy, he then pressed them into giving him a personal bodyguard for protection. This they did, and Peisistratus promptly used it to take over the city!

"When I heard of this, I at first resisted him and all that he stood for. Indeed, after spending a few years in power, he was exiled from the city. But now, children, I have come to see things differently. This Peisistratus is a wild man, a rabble-rouser, what we in Greece call a demagogue. He riles the people up with his words and plays on their passions. And yet, at the same time, he is not exactly a tyrant. Even after taking over the government, he respected the councils I set up and even allowed the juries to remain. I believe that he truly loves this land and its people and would do well by them. He's dangerous, for sure, but he may be our only hope.

"I have come up here to the hill country to encourage him to seize power again. Athens lacks vision, and Peisistratus is the only man left in this strife-torn land who has it. But now that I am here, I feel in my bones that I shall not live to guide him. Children, you must go in my place; you must watch Peisistratus and see that he follows the way of justice and of temperance. He's mighty clever, this self-appointed champion of the people; you must help him to channel that cleverness and use it to secure the freedom of Athens.

"Peisistratus lies just over that hill. There is no need for me to describe him to you. You'll recognize him when you see him. For me, the end of life has come. Children, help me to sit down. Here shall I die, and here you must bury me. If only, before I go, I can remember …"

"Remember what?" asked Alex.

"The words of a poem that Daniel taught me while I was in Babylon. I have written many poems in my life, but none have been as beautiful as those lines taught me by Daniel."

"Try to remember," said Stacey, "I'm sure the words will come back to you."

"Yes, yes," said Solon, "They *are* coming back: 'I know … that my … redeemer liveth, and that he shall stand at the latter day upon the earth: and though after my skin worms destroy this body, yet … yet …'"

"'Yet in my flesh shall I see God.'" Those last words were spoken by Stacey, though she could have sworn she had never memorized the verse. The words just came.

"Stacey," said Alex quietly, "Solon is dead. It is our duty now to bury him. Let us do it in the shade of that olive tree over there."

Slowly, sadly, the two children walked over to the olive tree, where they found, wonder of wonders, two shovels leaning against it. Neither child bothered to ask where they had come from. They just took them in hand and dug out the grave.

When they were done, and the body of Solon lay peacefully under the earth, Stacey turned to Alex and asked him to say a few words. Without planning it, without even thinking about it, Alex opened his mouth, and the words poured out: "I am the resurrection, and the life: he that believeth in me, though he were dead, yet shall he live …"

Chapter 9

The Rabble-rouser

When Solon had told the children that they would recognize Peisistratus when they saw him, he wasn't kidding! No sooner did Alex and Stacey turn the top of the hill than they saw a large, powerfully built man with a mass of curly black hair. He was waving his hands in the air and speaking in a loud, booming voice. At first the children thought that he must be addressing a great crowd, but as they positioned themselves behind the wildly gesticulating figure, they realized that Peisistratus was alone. His "audience" was not a group of Athenians citizens, nor even a party of shepherds, but a flock of fleecy white sheep.

"Alex," whispered Stacey, "I think this guy is a little bit crazy."

"I'm not sure, Stacey," said Alex, "Solon *did* say he was clever. Maybe he's practicing a speech to give before the Council. Let's get closer so we can hear him."

As it turned out, Alex and Stacey did not have to get much closer. Peisistratus had the kind of voice that could be heard and understood distinctly across the space of half a football field. He knew just which words to emphasize and how to organize his phrases so that they would fall on the ear like music. Here is some of what the children heard:

"Listen to *me*, O Athenians, and I shall tell you the way to save this city that we all love so dearly. I am not like these rich men here who claim to have your interests at heart but care only for fattening their own bellies. I am one of you: your struggles are my struggles; your dreams are my dreams. I am not one of them. My true father is Solon, he who gave us our democracy as a gift; my true mother is Athena, she who gave us our first Court of Justice. Put your trust in me, friends, and I will restore order and prosperity to Athens. And I will do it without taking power away from the people. I shall not be your king or your tyrant, as some of my enemies would have you believe, but your first citizen …"

Peisistratus suddenly stopped speaking and spun around. "Who is there?" he cried out, pulling a sharp sword from his side, "Who is trying to sneak up on me? If you are one of my enemies, then prepare to taste my blade in your belly."

"Don't worry," yelled Alex, who had slipped behind a rock, "We are not your enemies. We are two children sent here by Solon to help you retake Athens. My name is Alex, and this is my sister Stacey."

The Rabble-rouser

"Sent by Solon, you say?" answered Peisistratus, "but why did he not come himself?"

"Alas, Peisistratus," said Alex sadly, "the great Solon is dead. My sister and I buried him with our own hands. But before he died, he made us promise to help you. He warned us that you were a bit wild, but he also said that you were Athens' only hope."

"He was a wise and noble man. I mourn his passing as I would that of my own father. But what could you two children possibly do to help me ... Wait a minute! Stacey, what is that on your shoulder?"

"It's the owl of Athena," said Stacey, "She told us that it would keep us safe."

"You two children know Athena as well? You are strange children, indeed! The next thing you'll do is tell me you were there when Athena established our first Court of Justice."

"Well, as a matter of fact, Peisistratus ..."

"No, don't say it!" cut in Peisistratus, "I don't want to know! I'm a practical man and am only capable of believing so much. But I do believe what I see with my eyes, and I would swear before the Court of Justice itself that that owl on Stacey's shoulder is the sacred owl of the goddess Athena."

"It is," cried Stacey, "It is! But why does it interest you so much, Peisistratus?"

"Well, as I'm sure Solon told you, I'm a man who is not afraid to take big risks if the rewards are great. And as I look on that blessed owl, I see a chance—crazy as that chance may be—to take back control of Athens. Alex, are you strong enough to carry Stacey firmly on your shoulders?"

"Yes," said Alex, "I think I am."

"Good. We shall sit Stacey on your shoulders and put a large cloak over both of you. Then, I shall make up Stacey's face to look like that of Athena. It won't have to be perfect. When the people of Athens see the owl perched on her shoulder, they won't need to look too closely at her face. They will be too excited by the thought that the goddess has entered their city to ask too many questions. I've discovered that people often believe what they want to believe, especially if it is in their interest to believe it."

"But Peisistratus," said Alex, "What are you planning to do?"

"Not far from this place," explained Peisistratus, "I have hidden a silver chariot with a powerful horse to pull it. We shall make up Stacey to look like Athena and have her, or should I say Alex, stand beside me in the chariot. Then I shall drive it to Athens. No one who sees Athena next to me will dare to stop me. I wouldn't be surprised if I were able to drive the chariot right into the center of the marketplace."

"That's a great idea," said Alex, "Now I understand why Solon told us you were clever. I just hope Stacey doesn't fall off my shoulders when the chariot bounces on a stone!"

As it turned out, Alex's fears were groundless. Peisistratus was such a good charioteer that the children felt as if they were gliding along on a cloud. It was still a little bit scary for Alex, since the long cloak that Peisistratus had thrown over the two of them prevented him from seeing anything, but Stacey … Stacey was having the time of her life. With her head held high and her shoulders rolled back, Stacey played the part of the goddess with great flair and relish. Each time they passed someone on the road, Stacey would look down and bow her head slightly. Though she was dying to laugh, or at least to smile, she kept her lips firmly pressed together so that she would look as regal as possible. Even the owl played along and puffed out its feathery chest for all to see. All around them, the children could hear shouts of praise and of amazement:

"The goddess has come to us."
"Now Athens shall be great!"
"We are your servants, Athena."
"Bless us, O goddess."
"We are your people."

Meanwhile, as Stacey continued to nod her head, Peisistratus cried out in his loudest voice: "Citizens of Athens, I bring your goddess home to you. Run ahead of the chariot and tell the Council to prepare the city for her coming. Let the streets be filled with garlands and the altars anointed with oil. Athena has returned and has chosen me to set all to right."

The effect of Peisistratus' words on the people was immediate. Like children on Christmas morning who leap down the stairs and trip over rugs and tables in hopes of reaching the tree first, the people dropped their plows and their knitting and their pottery and went scurrying off to the city. By the time Peisistratus and the children had reached the marketplace, the city was packed with people singing and praising at the top of their lungs. The rich men on the Council tried to calm the crowd, tried to tell them it was all a hoax, but they were quickly shouted down. Eager for a word from the goddess, they pressed their bodies around the chariot and looked upward with hopeful faces. Instead of speaking, however, Stacey lifted the sword that Peisistratus had given her and swung it three times around his head.

The people cheered, and the owl let out a double hoot and flapped its wings wildly.

"Oh no," thought Alex to himself when he heard the hoot, "not again!"

✦ ✦ ✦

"Children, children," said the voice of Peisistratus, "wake up. It will be dawn soon, and it would not be good for the people to see you here."

"What?" said Alex and Stacey together, "Where are we?"

"You are in the temple of Athena. But there is no time for explanations. Take my hand, and I will lead you to my home."

"How long have we been gone?" said Alex, after they had all eaten a good breakfast and were resting comfortably in Peisistratus' sitting room.

"It has been six months since I last saw you," said Peisistratus, "I still marvel at how you were able to slip away from the chariot. One minute, Stacey was spinning the sword above my head; the next minute, both of you were gone and only my empty cloak was left in the chariot. However you did it, it certainly had a great effect on the crowd. When they saw you disappear into thin air, they were convinced that you were the real Athena. After that, I had no problem seizing control of the government."

"*Seizing* control?" said Alex with a suspicious look.

"Do not worry, young Solon," said Peisistratus, "I did not kill anyone. On the contrary, I have restored the democracy and continued the reforms begun by Solon. I have even ordered that a thousand olive trees be planted and that the pottery works be increased. I have set it as my goal to make Athens a center of trade and commerce. I have even honored Solon's wish to bring new citizens to Athens; last month, I sent out a general invitation to the best craftsmen in Greece to join us here and to use their skills to enrich both themselves and our city."

"I'm glad to hear it," said Alex, "I guess Solon was right when he said that you would honor his reforms and make Athens great. But I think there is one thing you have forgotten. Do you mind if I make a suggestion?"

"Certainly you may!" said Peisistratus, "I wouldn't be where I am if it were not for the help given to me by you and your sister. Tell me what is on your mind."

"Well," said Alex, "the last time my sister and I came to Greece—it's a long story!—we helped make sure the Trojan War happened in the right way so that Homer would one day be able to write the *Iliad* and the *Odyssey*. When we met with Athena, she told us that Homer's two poems were known by many in Greece and that they had the power to lead all who read them in the path of virtue."

"Yes, Alex, I know the poems well, but in one detail, you are mistaken. You speak of the poems as though they had been written down for all to read. They have not. Those in Greece who know the *Iliad* and *Odyssey* know them by ear, not by eye. After Homer's death, he was succeeded by a school of rhapsodes who wander throughout the Greek world reciting the poems from memory. While I was in exile from Athens, I even heard one of the rhapsodes sing for us the tragic tale of the death of Hector. I must tell you that even I shed tears at the telling; and yet, my tears were transformed into wonder and joy when the rhapsode sang of how Achilles put aside his wrath and gave back the body of Hector to his father, King Priam. Indeed, children, when I heard it, I vowed that I too would put aside my wrath against Athens and seek after a higher vision and calling."

"Yes," said Alex, "Yes! That's exactly my point. If you, Peisistratus can be moved and transformed by the poems, then others can be as well. You must not only bring trade and commerce to your city; you must bring Homer as well."

"I have an idea, Peisistratus," said Stacey, "Every year, our Daddy throws a big Christmas party for the boy scouts in Alex's pack, and during the party, he always has the boys act out the Christmas story while he plays carols on the piano. Maybe you could throw a big party every year, and during the party, you could bring some of those rhapsodes to Athens and have them recite the whole *Iliad* and *Odyssey*."

"Great idea, Stacey!" said Alex, "I'll bet the kids of Athens would love it too, because they could all stay up late and listen to the stories!"

"Stacey," said Peisistratus, "your idea is better than great—it's colossal. It will make Athens the envy of Greece. Yes, I will do as you suggest, but it won't be just a party: it will be a festival for all of Attica. We shall call it the Panathenaea (pan a thi NAY ah), and we shall dedicate it to the goddess Athena. We shall invite the whole world to attend. Businesses will close down, the Council will stop meeting, and the city will be decorated from end to end. I will give out free food and wine to everyone and shall put together a grand procession to march across Athens from the gate of the city to the temple on the Acropolis. And the centerpiece of the festival will be the reciting of Homer to all the people. No matter how long it takes, I will instruct the rhapsodes to recite both poems from beginning to end."

"That sounds like a lot of work," said Alex.

The Rabble-rouser

"It does indeed," said Peisistratus, "I hope you won't be upset, Stacey, but I think we better hold the festival every fourth year, rather than every year."

"That sounds OK to me," said Stacey, "but what about the *Iliad* and *Odyssey*? What if the rhapsodes begin to forget the words? Shouldn't you try to write it down?"

"Truly you have been given the wisdom of Athena," said Peisistratus, "I should have thought of it myself. In conjunction with the festival, I shall hire the best scribes to listen to the rhapsodes and record their words. As her gift to the rest of Greece, Athens shall be the first city to preserve a written copy of Homer. Yes, and by the writing down of Homer, I hope to inspire our own Athenian poets to compose their own great works. This vow I take: by the end of my life, Athens shall have grown not only into a center of trade but a center of culture as well. Here in this city, the mind and imagination shall be set free to explore and to grow. Homer's two poems shall become the main textbook in all our schools. The children of Athens shall drink in the tales of Troy as if they were mothers' milk, and, when they have grown to manhood, they shall build a new Golden Age. And the center of that Golden Age shall not be the Mycenae of Agamemnon, but the Athens of Solon and Peisistratus!"

"Hooray," shouted Alex and Stacey, "Let's get started right away."

✦ ✦ ✦

The next few weeks were busy ones for Peisistratus and the children, but they were also great fun. Like their parents, Alex and Stacey were good hosts and knew how to put on a good party. In fact, often times when their parents threw a party in Houston for their friends, Alex and Stacey would throw their own little party for the children of those friends! Alex's job was to figure out the order of the great procession and what types of flags and banners the soldiers would carry. He also helped choose the music they would play as they marched up to the Acropolis. Stacey, meanwhile, chose all the colors and all the flowers and decided what kinds of clothes everyone would wear. She was very particular about what she wanted.

When the dawn of the long-awaited day finally came, Alex and Stacey walked out the front door of Peisistratus' home to see the city of Athens transformed into a fairyland. The normally quiet streets were already bustling with crowds from all over Greece. Singing and laughter hung on the air, and the smell of fresh-baked bread was everywhere. It was like walking through a dream. Greece may have been broken up into a hundred different city-states, but here, for this day at least, they had left behind their squabbles and their divisions. They were all Greeks, fellow heirs of the heroic poems of Homer and of the great warriors who had sailed to Troy to fight in the legendary war. For awhile, even the division between rich and poor did not seem to matter. They were all involved in the same great adventure, and they had all been called to a higher vision of virtue.

The children, if truth be told, did not really think that the crowd would be able to listen to the long poems of Homer without getting bored and restless. But they were wrong. From the moment the rhapsode began the first line of the *Iliad*, a hush fell over the crowd, and all the people listened with rapt attention. Alex wasn't sure if the rhapsode would speak or sing; as it turned out, he did something in between. As someone strummed on a lyre, the rhapsode chanted the words to a set rhythm that sounded like the waves rising and falling against the shore. Alex and Stacey had, of course, lived through Homer's tales and experienced them first hand; yet, they too were hypnotized by the power of the rhapsode's song.

"Alex," whispered Stacey, after the rhapsode had finished reciting the scene when Hector says his final farewell to his wife and child, "look at the faces of the crowd. It's as if Hector were speaking to *them*. Can you see the tears in their eyes?"

"Yes, Stacey," said Alex, "I see them. It's as if they're realizing something about husbands and wives and parents and children that they never understood before. They've forgotten that Hector is the enemy; now they see him as a man with a family who loves him. I never knew that so many people could be moved and changed by a poem. Maybe Daddy was right when he told us once that the pen is mightier than the sword. I guess stories and poetry really *do* matter."

Once again, the children fell silent. They were one now with the crowd and neither of them felt like speaking. They just listened: not with their ears, but with their hearts. In fact, they listened so intently to the rhapsode that they did not even hear the hoot of the owl as it jumped on Stacey's shoulder and began to flap its wings.

Chapter 10

The Regicides

"Hey," yelled Stacey, when she had recovered from her "time-leap," "what's going on? We're still in the same place."

Stacey was correct. Despite the fact that they had just been catapulted through time by Athena's owl, the two children were sitting in the exact same spot listening to the exact same rhapsode recite the exact same portion of the *Iliad*. The Panathenaea was still going on, and the crowd was just as large as it had been before.

"You're right, Stacey," said Alex, "This doesn't make sense. Did we leap forward or didn't we? Everything looks exactly the … Hold on a minute! Look over there, Stacey."

Alex pointed with his finger to a royal throne just to the right of the stage where the rhapsode stood. The last time the children had looked at the throne, Peisistratus had been sitting on it, with his head held high and his chest thrust forward. But now there was a different man sitting on the throne, a younger man who looked like Peisistratus but whose eyes were much colder and crueler.

"This is strange," said Alex, "We must find out who that man is on the throne. It may not be safe, Stacey, but I'm going to ask someone in the crowd."

And with that, Alex turned to the man beside him and asked him if he knew the name of the person sitting on the throne.

"You must be a stranger to our city to ask such a question," said the man, "He who sits on the throne is Hippias (HI pee us), the tyrant of Athens."

"But isn't Peisistratus the king?" said Alex.

"Young man," said the stranger, "you must be getting your information from a liar or a fool. Peisistratus has been dead for fourteen years. The man on the throne is his son and heir, though he is as different from his father as darkness is from light. He rules Athens with an iron fist and ignores the cries of the people. If you look beside him, you will see his younger brother, Hipparchus (hi PAR kus). He, like his father, is of a nobler type. It is he who has organized this festival and who loves poetry and the arts with the same fervor as his father. Would that he were our king and not his brother. I fear that Hippias shall destroy this democracy of ours."

"Thank you, stranger," said Alex, taking Stacey by the hand, "it's time I took my sister home to bed."

"I'm not tired," said Stacey, when they had broken away from the crowd.

"I'm not really taking you home, silly," said Alex, "I just wanted an excuse to leave our seats. We *must* try to speak with Hippias and Hipparchus. Perhaps we can convince them to rule Athens as their father did."

"Alright," said Stacey, "but we better be careful. I don't like the look of that Hippias fellow at all."

With that, Alex and Stacey began to circle their way around the crowd so as to get behind the throne of Hippias. It wasn't an easy thing to do, for the festival was in full swing, and there were people everywhere. The shouts, the smells, the bright colors—all seemed intent on distracting the children from their purpose. Still, they pressed on. Finally, just when Alex was about to give up all hope of getting to Hippias, he spied a narrow alleyway that was empty of people and that seemed to curve in the direction of the throne.

"Let's duck in here, Stacey," said Alex, "I think it could be a shortcut."

Alex, who had always been good at mazes, was right about the alleyway. If they followed it around for another hundred yards, it would lead them directly to the throne. Excited that they were so close to their goal, the children began running very quickly; however, because they were afraid that they might trip on the cobblestones, they both looked down at their feet as they ran. It was for that reason that they did not see the two young men hiding in the shadows near the back of the alley. And because they did not see them, they ran right into them.

The impact startled Stacey so much that she opened her mouth to scream. Immediately, before the slightest sound could escape her throat, the taller of the two men clamped his large hand over Stacey's mouth. The second man did the same to Alex.

Then, with their free hands, the two men motioned to Alex and Stacey that they would let them go if they swore not to make a sound. The children nodded their heads in agreement, and the men released their hold.

"Who are you," whispered Alex, "and what are you doing in this alley?"

"We are two citizens of Athens," said the taller man, "My name is Harmodius (har MOE dee us) and my friend is Aristogeiton (a ris toe GY ton). We have come here this day to put an end to the life of Hippias the Tyrant. Too long have we and our fellow citizens suffered under his arrogance and his lust for power. It is time that we took matters into our own hands. We are not the only young men of Athens who feel this way, but it is we who have sworn to kill this tyrant no matter the cost to ourselves."

"No," said Stacey, "you must not do this thing. My brother and I are also on our way to Hippias, but we wish to talk to him, not kill him. Perhaps we can convince him to return freedom to the people and to rule as his father did."

"The time for words is long gone by," said Aristogeiton, "What we need now is action. Athens will have no more to do with kings, whether they be tyrants or not. It is we the people who are the true rulers of Athens, not the sons of Peisistratus."

"Please," said Alex, "let us at least try! If Solon were here, I do not think he would agree with your plan. He would bless you for your courage, but he would say that you lacked wisdom and temperance."

"Do not speak to us of Solon, boy," said Aristogeiton, "It is in his name that we plan to do this deed. He is the father of our democracy, and we are here to defend that democracy with our lives."

"But today is the Panathenaea," said Alex, "It is a day for celebration, not for killing."

"Exactly," said Harmodius, "what better day to celebrate freedom from our oppressors!"

Alex was about to speak again, to make a third attempt to stop them from carrying out their plan, but before he could, Harmodius and Aristogeiton stuffed rags in their mouths and tied their hands with two cords that they wore around their togas. Then, without saying a word, they slipped around the corner.

Alex and Stacey struggled to break the cords, but they did not have the strength. After what seemed like hours, but was really only five minutes, they heard a terrible cry coming from the center of town. The cry was followed by the shouts of hundreds of men and the sounds of scurrying feet. It was as if the city were under attack. Desperate to find out what was happening, the children tried again to break their cords, but they were just too tight.

Then, as if a light bulb had flashed in her head, an idea struck Stacey. Mustering all her strength, she lifted up her hands as high as they could go and twitched her right shoulder. When she did that, Athena's owl, who had been sleeping soundly, woke up and began to peck at the cord with its beak. In no time at all, the powerful beak of the owl had cut the cord in half. Stacey quickly freed herself and then helped Alex do the same. The next minute, they were running with all their might down the alley.

Needless to say, when they had reached the center of town—what the Athenians called the marketplace or agora (a go RAH)—the children found that the throne of Hippias was empty and that the rhapsode had stopped singing. All around them, people were yelling:

"Hipparchus is dead! Hipparchus is dead! Harmodius and Aristogeiton have stabbed Hipparchus to death."

"Hipparchus?" said Stacey, "I thought it was Hippias they wanted to kill."

"It was, Stacey," said Alex, "They must have made a mistake. They have killed the good man and left the bad one alive. I knew that their plan was a foolish one. I wonder what will happen to them now?"

Alex did not have to wonder for long. The supporters of Hippias and Hipparchus, who had carefully scattered themselves throughout the crowd, cried out loudly for revenge:

"Death to the regicides! Death to the king-killers!"

"Let us make examples of Harmodius and Aristogeiton!"

"All saw their criminal deed. There is no need for a trial."

The voices prevailed, and, as Alex and Stacey watched with horror, the chained bodies of Harmodius and Aristogeiton were dragged to the center of the agora. Hippias, who had been hiding behind a regiment of armed soldiers, stepped forward and struck the two assassins with the back of his hand.

"Execute them immediately," he ordered, "They are not fit to live."

Ignoring the angry murmurs of the crowd, four armed guards stepped forward and chained the regicides to two stone pillars that stood in the agora. Then, at a signal from Hippias, the rest of the soldiers drew their swords and rushed full speed at the chained prisoners.

"Long live the democracy! Long live freedom! Death to all tyrants!" shouted Harmodius and Aristogeiton as the soldiers drove their swords into their naked chests.

"Please owl," said Stacey, "I don't want to see any more of this. Please hoot and take us away from all this killing."

As if in response to Stacey's cry, the owl spun its head around and hooted twice, but the effect it had was not what Stacey had been expecting. Instead of the world around her going black, everything seemed to speed up. In fact, for a few moments, the crowd acted just like people do in a video when you push the fast forward button on your remote control. As Stacey looked on with amazement, every person in the agora began to scramble to and fro like mice being chased by a cat. The sight was so funny that Stacey almost laughed, but before she could, Alex grabbed her arm and yelled in her ear:

"Look, Stacey! Look at the bodies of Harmodius and Aristogeiton. They're moving."

Alex was right. As if by magic, the two young assassins had broken their chains and pulled themselves away from the stone pillars. At first, it seemed that they would run away, but instead they lifted up their right hands, each of which held a knife in its fist. They both let out a yell, but as they did, their faces froze and their lifted arms grew stiff. Their hair, which had been blowing in the wind, grew stiff as well and turned white. Their chests too and both of their legs grew equally rigid and changed their color from bronze to white.

"What's happening, Alex?" said Stacey.

"They're turning into statues. It's like the story of Pygmalion, but in reverse. The citizens of Athens must have carved the statues in memory of their deed. They were foolish, but they certainly were brave."

"How dare you call them fools," said a voice behind Alex, "They were great men, martyrs for freedom and democracy. We true Athenians shall never forget them."

The sound startled both Alex and Stacey. They had been staring so intently at the statues that they had not noticed that the agora had changed and was now populated by only a few people.

"I am sorry," said Alex, turning to the man behind him, "I only meant that their plan backfired on them. They killed the wrong man."

"Alas, young one, you speak the truth. After the death of Hipparchus, Hippias grew suspicious of everyone. Everywhere he turned, he saw plots and conspiracies. He killed many men in the four years after the death of his brother. But his madness only convinced the people of Athens that he, and all tyrants like him, must be overthrown. In fact, I can say with pride that it was my own family, the Alcmeonids (alk MAY oh nids), that helped to bring down Hippias.

"We knew that we could not overthrow Hippias alone, so we enlisted the aid of the Spartans. The Spartans, you should know, are a rather suspicious bunch. Before they do anything, they meet with the Oracle of Delphi to ask her advice."

"Yes," said Alex, "my sister and I once saw the Oracle. She is a prophetess who knows what will happen in the future."

"Exactly," continued the man, "she is a woman of great power and mystery, but the priests who work for her and interpret her prophecies are not so hard to understand. In return for some expensive gifts and a small chest of gold, we convinced the priests to tell any Spartan who visited the Oracle that before they did anything they must set Athens free. Well, after hearing this same message again and again for two years, the Spartans decided they had better act on it. They sent an army to Athens, and, with the cooperation of my family, sent Hippias and all his supporters into exile."

"I don't know if I like your methods any better than those of Harmodius and Aristogeiton," said Alex, "If you aren't careful, they may backfire on you as well!"

"I am grieved to say it," said the man, "but your words are true. The Spartans have now been in our city for the last two years, and have proven to be as great a danger to our democracy as Hippias was. In fact, this very day, the Spartan leaders have issued an order to exile every member of my family. Even worse, the Spartans have moved their troops into the Acropolis and have ordered that the People's Council be dissolved. Alas, it has been eighty-six years since Athens made Solon her supreme leader, and we are no closer now to fulfilling his dream than we were under Hippias."

"No," said Stacey, "it can't end like this. There must be something we can do, Alex."

"You bet there is!" said Alex, and with that he ran to the center of the agora and stood below the statues of Harmodius and Aristogeiton.

"Citizens of Athens," he cried out in his loudest voice, "Come to the agora! I have a word to speak to you that can only be spoken here, by the statues of your two martyrs for freedom."

A few citizens, startled by the sight of Alex and the serious tone of his voice, moved toward the center of the agora, but they were not enough. If Alex were to succeed in his plan, he would need to attract more listeners.

"Citizens!" he cried out more loudly, "I have been sent here to you by your goddess Athena to call you to action."

Still nothing. Stacey held her breath, and Alex shot a quick prayer to heaven.

And then the miracle happened.

With a powerful flap of its wings, the owl of Athena rose up from Stacey's shoulder and landed on the marble head of Harmodius. Then, with all the strength of its lungs, the owl began hooting and crying. This time, the sound did not draw Alex and Stacey away. Instead, it drew every true citizen of Athens to the agora.

"Yes," said Alex with a note of triumph in his voice, "this is indeed the owl of your goddess, sent here now to remind you of your inheritance. For almost a hundred years, you have enjoyed the benefits of the democracy given to you by Solon. Your city has prospered and has become the envy of all Greece. But have you been grateful? Have you sacrificed anything to keep that democracy alive? No, most of you have taken it for granted.

"Listen to me, my friends, last week I myself did not know what freedom was, nor why it had to be defended. But I have learned many things since then. I have learned that there are many out there who hate freedom and would crush it wherever and whenever it lifts its head. I have learned that freedom is not just something that happens: it takes wisdom on the part of its leaders and self-control on the part of its citizens. You have been given a great gift, Athenians. If you do not fight to preserve that gift, it will be lost to the world. If you do not fight, the sacrifices made by all those who came before you will have been made in vain.

"You have been chosen, Athenians, to bring back the Golden Age of Greece. Why should the virtues and glories of Homer's heroes be only things that we read about? I call upon you, young men, all you who grew up studying the *Iliad* and *Odyssey* in school, to march to the Acropolis and surround it with your bodies. *You are the heirs of Agamemnon and Achilles and Odysseus.*"

"Yes," shouted a young man in the crowd, "we are with you! Tell us what we must do."

"You no longer need me to tell you what to do," said Alex, "You are free men. You know what it is that you must do. You must lay siege to the Acropolis and to the Spartan soldiers stationed inside it. You must hold firm until they are forced by hunger to surrender their weapons and return control of Athens to the Council."

"Yes," shouted another in the crowd, "we shall kill every last Spartan."

"No," said Alex, "there has been enough killing. You must set them free and allow them to return to Sparta. Let them spread the message to all of Greece that Athens is free and that her citizens will no longer allow themselves to be controlled by tyrants from without or within. Today is your Independence Day, O Athens!"

Alex would have said more, but before he could speak again, a mighty wind rushed beneath his feet and lifted him off of the ground. Higher and higher the wind carried him until the agora looked no bigger than a sandbox and the people within it no bigger than ants.

"Alex," said Stacey, who was floating on the air beside him, "we're flying again. But I'm afraid that I've lost my owl."

"Don't worry, Stacey," said Alex, "I'm sure the owl has returned to Athena."

"I hope so," said Stacey, "I tried my best to take care of it. Do you think the Athenians will follow your advice and surround the Acropolis?"

"They will!" said a voice behind them, "The Spartan army will be expelled from Athens, and the democracy will be restored."

Alex and Stacey spun around in the air and saw, to their great joy and delight, the mighty, lion-clad figure of Hercules.

"Alex," he said, "what you have started today with your noble speech will lead Athens to perfect her laws and the way she runs her government. A whole new system will be created that will prevent future rivalry between the hill, plain, and coast, and that will help discourage envy and corruption amongst the classes. Athens and her democracy will finally come of age."

"Hercules," said Alex, "does that mean we can return to the battle of Thermopylae and that I can speak to Leonidas and tell him what we have learned about freedom?"

"Not quite yet, young Solon," said Hercules, "There are more things that you must see and learn before you can give your counsel to Leonidas. We must move ahead again in time to the year that the people of your world call 490 BC: ten years before the battle of Thermopylae. And we must move, as well, through space, from the West Coast of the Aegean (a GEE en) to the East Coast. That is to say, we must leave Greece behind and fly to Asia Minor, to those lands that the men of your day call Turkey, Iraq, and Iran."

"But why, Hercules," said Stacey, "why must we go there?"

"If you are to understand the Greek struggle at Thermopylae," said Hercules, "then you must understand something about the enemy. They call themselves the Persians, and, in the year toward which we are headed, they live under the tyranny of a powerful ruler named Darius (DA ree us); he it is who is the father of Xerxes. You must meet him, children, and learn the history of his people and why it is that he holds such hatred for the Greeks.

"But before we depart for Persia, I have one last thing to say to you. Thus far, I have called you children, but that time is now past. No longer are you children who must obey what you are told. Now that you have learned something of the true nature of freedom and have helped the Athenians to understand it themselves, I shall treat you as adults. Each of you, then, must decide for yourself whether you shall return to Texas or go on to Persia.

"Behold, with my club I shall draw a line of cloud along the blue sky that lies between you and me. If you step over the line toward me, then we shall soar together to Persia. But if you remain on your own side of the line, I shall return you home immediately. What then shall it be? Which path shall you choose?"

Without hesitating a moment, Alex and Stacey pushed themselves forward toward Hercules and crossed the line of cloud.

"Well done!" roared Hercules with a laugh in his throat, "Let us be off then. The future—and the past—await us!"

— Part —
2

East Versus West

Athens went from strength to strength, and proved, if proof were needed, how noble a thing freedom is, not in one respect only, but in all; for while they were oppressed under a despotic government, they had no better success in war than any of their neighbors, yet, once the yoke was flung off, they proved the finest fighters in the world.
—Herodotus

Chapter

11

In the Palace of Darius

Once Alex and Stacey had flown over the Aegean and looked down on the rugged coast of Asia Minor, they thought that their journey would soon be over. But they were wrong. Though the Persian Empire controlled the entire Ionian Coast, her capital city of Susa (SUE sa) lay one-thousand miles to the East. Even more impressive, from the former Lydian (LID ee an) capital of Sardis (located but a mere fifty miles from the coast) to Susa, the Persians had built a single, royal road to ensure speedy communication from the capital to the fringes of their massive Empire.

Alex, Stacey, and Hercules hovered for a moment above Sardis and then raced along the road as it winded up and down for over a thousand miles. They always made sure to stay high up, above the clouds, so that they would not be seen from the ground. As they flew, the children marveled at how much larger the Persian Empire was than Greece. For Greece to hold back the forces of Persia would be like the state of Texas defending itself in a war against the other forty-nine states. Of course, being true sons of Sam Houston, Alex and Stacey were convinced that Texas could easily win such a fight; still, as the seemingly endless Persian Empire stretched out below them, the children began to doubt the possibility of Greece surviving against such a mighty foe.

"I think I can read your minds, Alex and Stacey," said Hercules, "but do not despair. The lands of Persia are vast, but the people who serve in her army are mostly slaves. No slave fights as hard as a freeman; just so, a farmer who works his own land always gives more effort than the serf who works the land of another. Besides, each Greek who takes arms against Persia will be defending his country, his home, his family. Those in the armies of Persia fight only to win more land for a tyrant who has already over-extended himself.

"In case you are wondering, we are heading for the capital city of Susa…"

"Sousa!" said Alex, "you mean like John Philip Sousa!" Then, without waiting for a reply, Alex began to whistle "Semper Fidelis," his favorite piece to play on his cornet.

Hercules, who had never heard of John Philip Sousa and wouldn't have recognized the tune of "Stars and Stripes Forever,"

In the Palace of Darius

much less that of "Semper Fidelis," gave Alex a rather strange look and then continued:

"Though the Persian Empire boasts four different capitals, Susa is the grandest and lies at the heart of the other three. Darius always spends his winters here, and he has spared no expense in making it the most beautiful of the four capitals. He has personally overseen the layout of each room and tower and has imported the finest food and wine from around the world to entertain his guests. If you look down and ahead of you, you will see the citadel of Susa; it would take an army as large as that of Darius to tear down her fortifications."

By now, the three time (and space) travelers were hovering directly over the palace of Darius and could see the many rows of soldiers who guarded the walls of the citadel. Alex immediately began counting in his head the number of turrets and gates that he could see. Stacey, on the other hand, was interested in only one thing: the garden. Now, Stacey had seen courtyards before, many of which boasted a fountain and an array of different flowers. But never before had she seen one so richly decorated and so beautifully kept. The courtyard—or should I say the enclosed garden—of the palace was itself larger than Stacey's house in Houston and was home to a hundred varieties of birds and flowers and butterflies. Not one, but six fountains, each of a different shape and color, dotted the landscape. Under every tree and beside each flowering bush lay couches of gold and silver and ivory. Vines grew in every direction, their snaky fingers climbing up walls and wrapping around pillars, and yet none of the vines seemed wild or out of place. The garden was a magical blend of the natural and the artificial; every inch of it had been carefully planned to capture the abundance and vitality of nature without giving way to her disorder and decay. It was art, but it was a kind of art that concealed itself as nature.

As she gazed and gazed on the beauty and splendor of the enclosed garden, something that Daddy had told her once in passing came flooding back into Stacey's memory: paradise, that lovely word that we use to refer back to the Garden of Eden and ahead to the heavenly city, is actually a Persian word that means to wall around.

As gently as butterflies alighting on a twig, Alex, Stacey, and Hercules landed in the center of the garden behind a fountain of Poseidon, the Greek god of the sea. Aside from a few gardeners who were trimming the bushes and watering the flowers, the courtyard was empty.

"Here," said Hercules in a whisper, "I must leave you. Shortly, King Darius will appear. He is a shrewd and powerful ruler. You must be on your guard. Tell him as little as you can of your true purpose. Now, farewell."

Before Alex or Stacey could say anything in reply, Hercules soared back into the air and disappeared behind a cloud. Once again, they were on their own.

Normally, a situation like this would have left both children frozen with fear, but they were, thankfully, not given enough time to reach such a state. A mere two minutes after Hercules's departure, a tall figure in royal robes entered the garden from the north gate. Alex's first impression was that he looked more like an engineer or a bookkeeper than he did like a king. His eyes were small and very focused, as if he spent long hours pouring over maps and rows of numbers. His face had a calmness to it that made Alex think that it would take a great deal of prodding to make this man lose his temper. Everything about him was calculated; even

In the Palace of Darius

the way he paced the garden seemed to have an order and rhythm to it.

Alex allowed Darius to pace for ten minutes, but, when the king came near to the fountain of Poseidon for the third time, Alex stepped out boldly and bowed low.

"O mighty king of Persia," he said, "We have come."

"You have come?" said Darius, "But who are you? How did you get into the garden without being stopped by my guards?"

"Your majesty," said Alex, "we have been sent here by the Oracle of Delphi (DELL figh) to advise you on what is to come."

"The Oracle!" said Darius with a look of surprise in his eyes, "Well, if this be true, then you two are welcome visitors indeed. I am about to embark on a great campaign, and I would be grateful to have the advice of the Oracle. But if you two have traveled such a long distance, then you must be hungry and tired. I was about to take my dinner here in the garden; you two must join me as my guests."

Darius clapped his hands, and twenty servants immediately appeared from every corner of the palace. None of the servants dared look Darius in the eye, but kept their heads bowed at all times. Quicker than the children thought possible, the servants set up a table and three chairs beside the fountain of Poseidon and filled it with enough food to feed ten grown men. The dinner was delicious and left the children feeling sleepy and content.

When Darius could see that the children had eaten their fill, he clapped his hands again, and the plates disappeared. Alex, who, unlike his sister, liked things neat and orderly, marveled at the efficiency with which Darius ran his palace.

"O king," he said, "I can see that you are a man who likes things to be done properly."

"You have a keen eye, stranger," said Darius, "As I run my kingdom, so do I run my household. When I inherited the throne from my predecessors, the Persian Empire was unwieldy and difficult to manage. Fearing that such disorder would lead to chaos and civil war, I immediately gave orders that the kingdom should be divided into twenty regions. I call these regions satrapies (SAY trap ees) and over each of them I have appointed a satrap (SAY trap) to keep the peace and collect taxes. Children of Delphi, I firmly believe that Persia has been gifted with a great destiny, but there are very few in my kingdom who feel as I do. It is my hope that I can pass my vision down to my satraps, and, through them, to my people. Yet I fear that only a great struggle will fill them with a sense of the destiny of Persia."

"You sounded just like Solon when you said that."

"Solon?" said Darius, "Do you children know of Solon?"

"We don't know *of* Solon," said Alex, "We *know* Solon, or at least we knew him."

"But that is impossible," said Darius, "Solon died long before you two were ... well, these are strange days, and I have heard of even stranger things. Children, I was prepared to hear your story, but instead, I think that I shall tell *you* a story."

"Oh please do," said Stacey, "my brother and I both love stories."

"Very well then, I shall, but I warn you that it is a complex tale, woven of many threads. Still, as your friend Solon is the master thread that holds the rich tapestry together, I am confident that you shall find the tale to your liking."

Chapter

12

Look to the End

"Today," Darius began, "Persia is the ruler of the world. Her power and might extend from the Black Sea in the north to Egypt in the south, from the Aegean in the west to India in the east. But it was not always so. A hundred years ago, the lands of Persia were divided amongst many tribes and nations: Medes (MEEDS), Egyptians, Babylonians, Lydians, and before them the Assyrians. Each nation had its kings and queens, but of all the rulers who ever sat upon a throne, the greatest, the richest, the most splendid was Croesus (KREE sus) of Lydia. His wealth was legendary, as were his wisdom and hospitality.

"It is said that he once entertained in his palace at Sardis a man from Athens, and that after they had eaten their dinner, Croesus invited the man to visit his vaults and to take from them as much gold as he could carry. When the man heard this, he immediately took off the clothes he had been wearing and replaced them with a wide apron, a set of baggy pants, and a pair of high-topped boots that reached clear to his knees. Once in the treasury of Croesus, the man stuffed so much gold dust into the sides of his boots that he could hardly lift his legs. He did the same with the apron and the pants and even filled his mouth with gold dust. When he returned to Croesus, he looked more like a monster than a man: his stomach bulged out a foot in front of him, his cheeks seemed ready to burst, and his shoulders were hunched over from the tremendous weight of the apron. Croesus no sooner laid eyes on this parody of a man than he burst into a fit of laughter: 'You clever fool,' he cried, 'not only shall I give you all the gold you have upon you, but I shall give you as much gold again.'

"The name of the man was Alcmeon (alk MEE on), and with the riches he won from Croesus, he founded one of the richest families in Athens."

"So that's how the Alcmeonids got their start," said Alex, "I always thought they were too tricky for their own good. They even used some of their money to bribe the Oracle of Delphi into getting Sparta to help overthrow Hippias, the tyrannical son of Peisistratus."

"You don't say," said Darius, "It may interest you to know that this Hippias now lives in Persia and is one of my advisors—though I can't say that I always trust him. Perhaps you will meet him some day. But let me return to my tale:

"Soon after Alcmeon had sailed back to Greece, Croesus was visited by another Athenian who did not share Alcmeon's lust for wealth and power. His name, as I'm sure you've guessed, was Solon, and he had been lured to Sardis in hopes of meeting her famous king. Though Solon had just spent several months among the vast treasure houses of the Egyptians, he was unprepared for the magnificence of Croesus's palace. The Lydian King, pleased by the awe he read in the eyes of Solon, led his guest through every room of his palace and allowed him to inspect every object of value from the smallest chest of gold to the most priceless work of art. When the two had completed their tour, Croesus, who was not above a little vanity, turned to Solon and said: 'Master Solon, you who are famed for your wisdom, your poetry, and your travels throughout Greece and Asia, I would like to ask you a simple question. Of all the men you have met in your life, who would you say was the happiest?'

"Solon thought for a moment, and then replied: 'Of all the men I have met in my life, the happiest was an Athenian named Tellus.'

"'What!' said Croesus, who was shocked and a little bit upset that Solon had not named him as the most happy, 'I have not even heard of this man. Why do you call him the happiest?'

"'It is no surprise that you do not know his name, O mighty king. Tellus had neither great wealth nor great power, but he was a loyal and honored citizen of a great city. He had many sons and many grandsons, all of whom shared his honor and paid him respect. Tellus lived to a ripe old age with his full health and vigor intact and died fighting for Athens in a battle against one of her neighboring enemies. He even had the honor of being buried there on the battlefield.'

"As you can imagine, Croesus was not pleased with this answer, but, not wanting to insult his guest, he concealed his anger. Instead, he asked Solon to speak out the name of the second happiest man.

"'Here, my Lord, I will have to bend the rules slightly. Second place goes to two men, brothers of the same mother. Their names were Cleobis (KLEE oh bis) and Biton (BY ton), and they were citizens, not of Athens, but of Argos. They lived a moderate but comfortable life, and they were both famed throughout their region for their strength and athletic skill. But it was neither in a running race nor in an Olympic event that they proved their worth. Rather, it was something they did for their mother that won them lasting fame.

Eager to drive her ox-cart to a festival held in honor of Hera, the wife of Zeus, the pious mother of Cleobis and Biton left her home in search of her two oxen. But the oxen had strayed from their pasture, and the woman soon became frantic lest she be late for the festival. In answer to their mother's need, the two sons strapped themselves to the ox-cart and pulled it at top speed for six miles. When they had reached the city, the two young men, exhausted from the journey, lay down on the temple steps and slept. All of Argos praised their deed before their mother, and she, overjoyed, called upon the goddess to give her sons the greatest of boons. This Hera did. Cleobis and Biton never woke again, but died peacefully in their sleep, surrounded by the fullness of their fame. In their honor, the citizens of Argos erected two statues, one in the likeness of Cleobis, the other in that of his brother. These, O king, I call the most happy.'

"'Have you lost your mind, Solon?' cried Croesus, his patience brought to an end by Solon's strange replies, 'How can you consider these two brothers to be happier than I am? You have seen my wealth and walked the full length of my palace. How then can you deny me the title of most happy of men?'

"'O king, your riches and your power are beyond belief. Yes, for the moment, you are the happiest and most fortunate of men. But how can you or I know that your fortune will remain with you until the end of your days? No, no, Croesus, you must count no man happy until he is dead, for life is troubled and uncertain, and we none of us know what the morrow will bring. Some might have called me the happiest of men when the citizens of Athens chose me as their supreme ruler, but they would have been wrong. For look at me now: I am virtually an exile from my city, hated and envied by those very citizens whom I labored to save. Again I say to you, O king, if you are to judge a man's happiness, then you must look to the end. He who dies with his honor and fortune intact: he alone is to be given the title of happiest.'"

"Yep," said Alex, "that sounds like Solon!"

"It sure does," said Stacey.

"Children," said Darius, "you must not interrupt the tale. Still, I forgive you this time, for your interruption comes at a good moment. We must now leave behind Croesus and his kingdom of Lydia and turn our attention instead to a larger kingdom to the east: that of the Medes. While Solon was instructing Croesus in the ways of fate and fortune, the kingdom of Media was ruled by a man named Astyages (a STY a jeeze). As kings go, he was an able ruler, but he could be cruel and unjust to those he considered rivals.

"One night, this Astyages had a dream in which he saw a great vine shooting out from the belly of his daughter and stretching out to encompass all the lands under his rule. Interpreting the dream as a warning that his daughter's son would someday seize his throne, Astyages married off his daughter to a Persian named Cambyses (cam BY seeze). In those days, children, the Medes looked down upon the weaker Persians and despised them as slaves. Astyages thought, to his folly, that the son of a Persian could never be a threat to his throne. But when his daughter gave birth to a son and when Astyages' dream was repeated the following night, the King of the Medes decided he must take more forceful measures to ensure the safety of his throne.

"Accordingly, Astyages summoned his loyal servant and kinsman, Harpagus (har PAY gus) and commanded him to take the baby from his daughter and have it put to death. Harpagus agreed to carry out the evil deed, but when the time came to kill the infant, he found that he could not do it. Instead, he gave the baby to a herdsman named Mithridates (mith ri DAY tees) and ordered the herdsman to carry out the orders of Astyages. Mithridates agreed, but he too was stopped, not so much by compassion for the child as compassion for his wife. That very morning, the herdsman's wife had given birth to a child, but the child had died in her arms. Grief-stricken at the loss of her baby, the wife of Mithridates begged her husband to let her raise the grandson of Astyages as though he were their own child. Mithridates, seeing no harm in this deception, agreed to his wife's pleas.

"For the next twelve years, the child, whose name was Cyrus (SIGH rus), grew up in the home of the humble herdsman, ignorant of his royal birth. But the nobility of his blood soon showed itself. One day, Cyrus and his friends decided to play a game of make-believe. All the children voted and decided that Cyrus would be appointed as their king. No sooner was this choice made than Cyrus immediately began to give orders, all of which his friends obeyed without question. Indeed, if you could have watched those children play, you would have sworn that Cyrus had been a king all his life. But there was one child, whose father was a noble in the court of Astyages, who refused to follow the orders of the herdsman's son. When Cyrus learned this, he seized a hold of the nobleman's son and commanded that he be beaten by his friends. Not used to being treated in such a manner, the nobleman's son ran home to his father demanding that Cyrus be punished. Word of the incident soon reached the ears of Astyages, and he commanded that Cyrus be brought into his presence.

"Astyages expected that Cyrus would cower before him and beg forgiveness of the nobleman's son. But he did nothing of the sort. When confronted by Astyages, Cyrus insisted that all the children had chosen him as their king and that, in ordering his friends to beat the nobleman's insolent son, he had merely acted as any wise king who wished to hold the respect of his nobles and subjects would have done. Astyages was impressed by the boy's words and demeanor and realized at once that he could not be the son of a herdsman. He therefore questioned Mithridates and Harpagus closely until the full truth was revealed. Astyages forgave Mithridates, who had acted in ignorance, but nursed a silent revenge against Harpagus.

"One week later, Astyages invited all of his kinsmen to a banquet. He fed them all on the riches of meats, but to Harpagus, he served a special kind of meat reserved only for him. When Harpagus had finished his meal, Astyages asked him what he thought of the meat. Harpagus admitted that it was very tasty and asked what type of animal it had come from. In response, Astyages ordered his servants to bring forth a covered dish. Harpagus removed the lid, whereupon he found, to his horror, the head and the hands of his only son. 'Since you refused my order to kill my grandson,' said Astyages, 'I have decreed instead that you should devour your own son.'

"Knowing he could do nothing for the moment, Harpagus declared that Astyages had acted justly in the manner. But revenge burned deep in his heart, and, when Cyrus had come of age, Harpagus convinced the nobles of Persia to rally behind him and overthrow Astyages and the Medes. Thus, with the help of Harpagus, Cyrus seized the throne and made the Persians the new masters of the East. As king, Cyrus proved to be both strong and wise, and he greatly expanded the power and dominion of the Persians. No army could stand against him, and no monarch ever received such loyalty from his troops. Indeed, Cyrus did what few had ever dared try before; he laid siege to the great and ancient city of Babylon. Though the Babylonians had ruled a mighty nation for centuries, Cyrus stripped their power from them in a single night."

"Wait a minute," said Alex, "did you say Cyrus conquered Babylon?"

"I did," replied Darius.

"O king," said Alex, "forgive me for interrupting you again, but I must ask you a question. When Cyrus became master of the Babylonians, did he also become master of a people known as the Jews?"

"Yes," said Darius, "I know of these people. They are from a land known as Israel, and their capital city is called Jerusalem. At one time, they had a magnificent temple, but when the Babylonians seized control of the capital, they razed the temple to the ground. Though I could never determine why, when Cyrus defeated Babylon, he chose to allow these Jews to return to Jerusalem and to rebuild their temple; he even ordered that the building be paid for out of the royal treasury. I have seen the decree myself. In fact, children, out of respect for Cyrus's wishes, I sent, in the early days of my reign, royal letters to Jerusalem demanding that my governors assist in the rebuilding of the temple and prevent any hostile tribes from attacking the Jewish builders. Indeed, like Cyrus before me, I partly funded this work from my own treasury.

"They are a strange people, these Jews. They worship only one God and claim that He has delivered them again and again. They even claim that it was *their* God who anointed Cyrus to overthrow the Babylonians and restore the Jews to their land. As far as I know, they have also given credit to their God for *my* part in the restoration. In any case, it has now been a full twenty-five years since they completed the rebuilding of their temple, though I am told that the new one is but a pale shadow of the original. I am not a particularly religious man myself, but I have found it a wise policy to allow the different cultures that make up my empire to practice their religious rituals in peace."

"That is a wise policy," said Alex, "but forgive me for interrupting. Please continue your tale."

"To do so, I must step back seven years, for before he dared attack Babylon, Cyrus planned first to seize control of Lydia. This he did, defeating the armies of Croesus in a great battle. Had Croesus been wise, he would have avoided the battle and made a treaty of peace, but his own folly was his undoing. When he asked the Oracle whether he should resist Cyrus, the Oracle replied that if Croesus attacked Persia, he would destroy a great empire. Alas, too late did Croesus realize that the empire he would destroy would be his own.

"Cyrus, enraged at Croesus for daring to defy him, ordered that the deposed King of Lydia be tied to a stake and burned alive. His orders were obeyed immediately and only minutes later, Croesus could taste the smoke rising up from the fire. In a voice filled with pain and regret, the defeated Croesus cried out three times the name of Solon. Cyrus, hearing Croesus's lament and wondering who this Solon could be that his name should be the last thing on the dying king's lips, called out to Croesus to reveal to him the identity of Solon. And so, as the fire grew hotter and the smoke rose higher, Croesus told Cyrus of his meeting with Solon and of how the wise Athenian had taught him never to count a man lucky until he was dead. 'So you too, King of Persia,' concluded Croesus, 'may be today the strongest and most fortunate man in Asia, but who can say what your fate shall be in the years that follow. Look to the end, O king; I only wish that I had done so myself.'

"When Croesus had finished his story, Cyrus immediately ordered that the fire be put out and the life of Croesus spared. Unfortunately, his order came too late. The fire was raging too fiercely for Cyrus's men to approach it. Croesus seeing what was happening called out to Apollo to spare him. No sooner was the prayer out of his mouth than the clouds rolled in and the rains fell. The rain put out the fire, and Cyrus declared that from that day forth, Croesus would be his personal advisor. And thus it was that Solon, though dead and in his grave, saved the life of a Lydian king.

"With Croesus at his side, Cyrus went from victory to victory. In time, he died and was succeeded by his son, Cambyses, who conquered Egypt and brought it too under the control of the Persian Empire. Like his great-grandfather Astyages before him, Cambyses was a paranoid man. Fearing a dark prophecy, he had his brother Smerdis secretly put to death. Soon after, Cambyses himself died, and the wicked Magi (MA jy) …"

"Magi!?!" said Alex and Stacey together.

"Yes," said Darius, "the Magi are a race of people with ancient ties to the Medes. They are famous astrologers and interpreters of dreams. Cyrus and Cambyses consulted them often, as did Astyages before them. But as I was saying, the wicked Magi, seeing an opportunity to wrest power away from their Persian overlords, hatched a sinister plot. Since only a few people in the empire knew of the murder of Smerdis, the Magi dressed up one of their own men to look like Smerdis and then declared him King of Persia. But I, with the help of six other lords of Persia, foiled their plot and killed the false Smerdis. After much deliberation, the six chose me to be the new King of Persia and gave me the daughter of Cyrus as my wife. As such, I am the son-in-law of Cyrus, though I also count that same Cyrus as my cousin through the blood of my father. In Cyrus's name, I have expanded even further the might of the Persian Empire and have devised my system of satrapies for keeping peace and order throughout my entire realm. Above all, I have learned the lesson of Solon. Ever and always, I look to the end.

"But now, children, I fear that it is late; it is time for all of us to retire to our beds."

Alex and Stacey, who were by now quite sleepy, did not argue with Darius but headed straight for their room. They were both looking forward to a nice, long rest. But that rest was to be denied them.

Chapter 13

The Magi

"Alex," said Stacey, after the guards had led them to their room, "do you think everything that Darius told us was true?"

"I think what he *told* us was true," said Alex, "but I have the feeling that he was hiding something. You know the way adults talk when they only want you to know half the truth."

"Yes, Alex," said Stacey, "I had that feeling too. I'm going to peek out the door and see if the guards are still there."

With that, Stacey tiptoed over to the door and laid her hand on the latch. Slowly but firmly she pressed down on the latch. It wouldn't move! The guards had locked the door from the outside. The children were prisoners.

Before Stacey could speak, Alex sensed the truth and rushed over to her side. He too tried to press down on the latch, but it wouldn't budge an inch. He was all set to try again, when the sound of a faint click echoed across the room. For a moment, the children thought that the guards had returned and were unlocking the door: that is, until they realized that the click they had heard had come not from the door but from the opposite wall. Alex and Stacey held their breath and stared at the wall, but they could not identify the exact source of the click. The wall was solid with no doors or windows.

Or was it? As the children looked on with wonder and fear, a small piece of the wall, about three feet high and three feet wide, slid open, revealing a dark hole with a pin prick of light at its center.

"Children," said a hushed voice from the other side of the wall, "come quickly! Your lives are in danger. You must crawl through the hole and follow it toward the light. Do not be afraid. When you reach the light, you will be safe."

Normally, neither child would have even *thought* about entering that dark hole, but the voice sounded like a truthful one, and they both had decided by now that they could not trust Darius or his guards. And so, with Alex in the lead and Stacey right behind him, the two children pulled themselves into the hole. The very second Stacey's feet cleared the entrance, she heard the sound of the panel sliding shut behind her. There was no going back.

The inside of the hole, which was really a long, narrow shaft, had a dank, musty smell that made both of the children want to sneeze. Luckily, their fear of being heard far outweighed their desire to sneeze! The bottom of the shaft was hard and dusty and had several jagged edges that ripped a few holes in the children's clothes and tore at their hands and knees. Still, they pressed on toward the light that shone ever more brightly at the end of the shaft.

Finally, after what seemed an hour, Alex and Stacey dragged themselves out of the shaft and into a large room made of pure white marble with a gold trim running along the top and bottom and strange images of planets and stars painted on the walls. In the center was a stone table upon which rested an open book, a compass, and a single white candle: the source of the light which they had followed through the shaft. Three steps led up to the table and behind it there stood a throne of carved wood studded with diamonds and rubies. It took them less than a minute to realize that they were in some kind of a temple: a sacred, holy place of meditation, study, and prayer.

"Children," said a voice from the corner of the room, "I am so glad you have made it safely. I do hope your journey through the shaft was not too difficult. My name is Balthazar (BAL tha zar), and I am the leader of the Magi. You now stand in our most sacred chamber; not even Darius himself has been allowed to trespass."

"Thank you, Master Balthazar," said Alex, "Just before the panel in the wall slid open we had discovered that the guards had locked us in our room. In fact, the guards may have already realized that we are gone."

"Do not fear," said Balthazar, "you are safe here."

Relieved by Balthazar's words, Alex and Stacey took another look around the room. That was when Alex thought to gaze upward for the first time. What he saw made him grab Stacey's chin and tilt her head toward the ceiling.

"Look, Stacey, look," he said, "there is a huge glass window on the ceiling. You can see the stars through it. I think I even recognize the Big Dipper."

"You are very observant, young man," said the Magi, "That portal is our great window onto the starry heavens. Through it we watch the great dance of the constellations. If you look to your right, you will find a notched wheel. Turn it and see what happens."

Alex did as he was told, and, to his great surprise, he discovered that with each turn of the wheel, the portal moved an inch to the right.

"From here," said Balthazar, "we mark the movements of every planet and star. And in those heavenly bodies, we read the fate of nations and their kings. Indeed, it is those very stars that have foretold your coming and warned us of the danger to your lives.

"Children, you must not be fooled by Darius's praise of Solon. Above all peoples on earth, he hates the Athenians and would reduce all of them to slaves. Far to the west, along the coast of Asia Minor, there lie the Greek cities of Ionia, many of them originally founded by Greeks who left Athens in search of a new life. For many years, Ionia was controlled by the Lydians, but when Cyrus defeated Croesus, control of Ionia passed into Persian hands. At first, the Ionians were content to pay their taxes and give homage to Persia. But this Darius has grown too powerful for his own good. Assured by a prophecy that he is destined someday to rule both Europe and Asia, he has increased the taxes on the Ionians and has put them under the thumb of tyrannical satraps who rule in his name.

"Finally, the Ionians could take no more of Darius's pretensions and, nine years ago, broke out in open revolt. The center of the resistance was in the city of Miletus (my LEE tus), a city with ancient ties of blood and culture to Athens. Fearing that Darius' troops would crush them, the citizens of Miletus called to Greece for help. In response, Athens sent twenty war ships, along with five more from the neighboring city of Eretria (e RE tree a). With the help of the Greeks, the Ionians were not only able to inflict much injury on Darius and his troops, but marched into the interior of the Empire and sacked the city of Sardis. Eventually, the Persians regrouped and crushed the rebellious Ionians, but Darius has never forgiven the Athenians for their part in sacking Sardis and humiliating his army. Indeed, lest his anger not cool down, Darius has ordered his servants to say to him every night before he dines: 'Remember Athens!' You did not hear his servant say these words last night when you dined with Darius for they are no longer necessary. Tomorrow morning, Darius's generals, Datis (DAY tis) and Artaphernes (ar ta FER nees), are set to leave for the coast and from there to sail to Athens with a war fleet. Darius has sworn that before the year is out, Eretria and Athens will be brought to their knees and be forced to swear allegiance to Darius himself."

"So," said Alex, "that's what Darius was referring to when he told us he was about to embark on a great campaign. No wonder he was so happy to meet visitors from Delphi. I'll bet when he learned that we not only knew Solon but the Alcmeonids as well, he guessed that we were friends of Athens. I'm sure that when he told us Hippias was living in his court that we betrayed our hatred for him by the looks on our faces."

"Yes, you have guessed correctly. Indeed, your words lead me to the second piece of bad news that I must share with you. Datis and Artaphernes are to be accompanied on their expedition by none other than Hippias himself. Hippias, who is close in the counsels of Darius, has never forgiven the Athenians for sending him into exile, and he is determined before he dies to become tyrant of Athens once again. He has long conspired with Darius for this day, and Darius has promised that if he helps his generals to seize control of Athens that he, Hippias, will be allowed to rule the city in Darius' name. Thus you see, children, how the tyrants of West and East conspire together for the destruction of freedom.

"For, be ye not fooled, as much as Darius hates the Athenians for their part in the Ionian revolt, even more does he hate them for their freedom and their democratic ways. Darius, like Hippias, fears that if the idea of freedom that was born in Athens were to spread throughout Persia that he, and all tyrants like him, would be dashed from their thrones. Indeed, he blames Athenian ideas for inspiring the Ionians into thinking that they could possibly break away from the control of Persia."

"I thank you again, Balthazar," said Alex, "for sharing these things with us, but what are we to do now?"

"All has been arranged, children," said Balthazar, "This very night, my fellow Magi will smuggle you in baskets into the caravan of Datis and Artaphernes as it travels along the thousand-mile royal road from Susa to Sardis. From there, others will help you to stowaway on the lead warship and sail with them in secret to Greece. It is my hope that, with the help of that God who made the heavens and their brilliant lights, you will be able to reach Athens before it is too late and warn them of the invasion."

"You have been so kind to us, Balthazar," said Alex, "that I wish there were some way that we could repay you."

"Tell them about the star, Alex," said Stacey, "the Star of Bethlehem."

The Magi

Alex thought for a moment and then spoke out in the gravest voice he could muster: "Master Balthazar, I can tell that you are a man who likes mysteries and riddles. In return for your kindness, then, I shall tell you a riddle—one that you must write down in the books of the Magi and preserve for the next five-hundred years. One day another anointed one shall rise, one like unto Cyrus. For just as Cyrus, the son of a king, was raised as the son of a herdsman, another will come some day who is more than a son of the king, who is, in fact, the Son of the God who made the heavens. Like Cyrus, he will be raised as a poor man, the son of a humble carpenter, but to those who have eyes to see and who know how to follow the light of the stars, he will be revealed in all his kingly splendor. So keep watch on the night sky, O leader of the Magi. Some day your descendants shall see his star rising. When they do, they must follow it wherever it leads, just as my sister and I followed your candle through the darkness of the shaft. Their journey, like our own, will be long and hard, but at the end a great prize will await them. Then shall East and West be united as one!"

"You are a strange young man," said Balthazar, "I fear that you are Apollo in disguise. I shall surely write down your words and keep them in the sacred books of the Magi. Perhaps in the years to come, you and your riddle shall prove to be a candle shining in the darkness of tyrants like Darius and all the madness of war.

"But come now, I have beds prepared for each of you that you may sleep for a few hours. When the dawn rises tomorrow, you will need to be alert. A long and dangerous journey lies ahead of you. May all the lights of the heavens shine down on your going forth."

Chapter

14

The Invasion

The next three months, as Alex and Stacey were carried along the royal road from Susa to Sardis, were both frightening and exhilarating. The Magi were clever and well organized and were there to help the children at every step of their journey. Still, during the days that the caravan moved from city to city, Alex and Stacey were very much on their own. In the beginning, they spent most of those days hiding in baskets, but as their courage and hunger increased, they grew more bold. Alex was quite a good cornet player, and so it only took him a few hours to figure out how to play the much cruder trumpets and horns that accompanied the Persian caravan. Stacey, meanwhile, remembering her five years of ballet, joined the belly dancers who performed for the soldiers every evening. As you might imagine, the two children soon become favorites amongst the musicians, the dancers, and the fighting men; all marveled that the children had such skill for their age. Alex and Stacey both loved the applause, and Stacey loved even more the beautiful costumes she got to wear when she danced.

Once the children had managed to become a part of the life of the caravan, the days began rushing by more quickly; before they knew it, the three-month journey from Susa to Sardis had been completed, and, but a few short days after that, they found themselves on the Ionian Coast boarding the war ships for their voyage to Greece. As it turned out, they did not need the Magi to help smuggle them aboard. By then, the children had become so popular that Datis and Artaphernes themselves invited them to sail on board the lead ship where they could entertain the officers with their playing and dancing.

The first few days of the voyage were uneventful, but, on the third day, the war ships landed on the island of Naxos. Here it was that Alex and Stacey got their first taste of Persian cruelty. Though Naxos was a small, peaceful island in the middle of the Aegean Sea, and though the islanders offered no resistance, the Persian fleet sacked the city, burnt its temples to the ground, and dragged its people off to slavery. They did the same to many other islands, punishing severely all those that would not pledge to help Persia in her invasion of Athens.

One night, after the fleet had captured yet another island and forced its young men to serve in the Persian navy, Alex and Stacey found that they could not sleep. Quietly, they stole up to the deck to get a breath of fresh air. There was no moon that night and a bank of clouds covered most of the stars. Fearing that it was too dark to walk safely on the deck, Alex and Stacey turned around and began groping their way back down to the sleeping quarters. It was at that moment that Alex saw, out of the corner of his eye, a small light appear on the deck. At the same moment, Stacey heard someone whisper the names of Datis and Artaphernes. Hoping they might overhear something important, the children crouched down on the steps and strained their ears to follow the conversation.

"Hail, noble Persians," said the voice, "Our day of victory is at hand. Very soon now we shall land on the island of Euboea (you BEE a), which stretches its long, skinny body along the eastern coast of Greece. As soon as we land, we must head directly for the city of Eretria. The Greeks are divided and will not be able to pull together fast enough to defend Eretria from our troops. Once Euboea falls, it will not be difficult to march southwest toward Attica. Midway between Eretria and Athens lie the flat plains of Marathon, a perfect place for our cavalry to mount their attack. With Eretria defeated and Marathon in our hands, it will be a small matter to seize control of Athens."

"Thou art a wise counselor, O Hippias," said Datis, "We are lucky to have with us one who knows so well the geography of Greece. Once we have taken Eretria, you shall lead us yourself to Marathon. I would not be surprised to see you sitting on the throne of Athens within the week."

"That shall be a great day indeed," said Hippias, "It will take me but a few days to crush their democracy and convert Attica into a satrapy of Persia."

"I applaud your resolve, Hippias," said Artaphernes, "but do you think the Athenians will fall so easily? Can they really be as weak as you suggest?"

"You have nothing to fear from the Athenians," said Hippias with scorn, "Their freedom has made them soft; they care more for their luxuries and their festivals than they do for the sword and the spear. Without a strong leader like Darius to hold them together and give them orders, each Athenian thinks only of his own business and his own profits. Attack them, and they will scatter—like sheep without a shepherd."

"So, Hippias," said Artaphernes, "you blame their weakness on their love of freedom."

"I do," said Hippias, "The common herd are no more fit for freedom than are children. It is the proper way of nature that one should rule the many. To offer freedom to the people is to encourage lawlessness and to spread discontent. People don't want to have to make choices of their own; they just want to be told what to do."

"But what of their laws?" said Datis, "I have heard that the Athenians respect the law as a thing higher than their rulers."

"That's all nonsense," said Hippias, "started by a most malicious liar named Solon. He even bewitched my father, Peisistratus, into believing his foolish ideas. What the people need is an iron fist. They simply cannot be trusted to make proper decisions for themselves."

When Hippias had finished speaking, it was all Alex could do to stop Stacey from rushing on to the deck and pushing Hippias overboard.

"Let me at him," whispered Stacey, "Why did we ever try to stop Harmodius and Aristogeiton from killing Hippias? I'd like to go over there and punch him in the nose."

"Be patient, Stacey," said Alex, "there's nothing we can do for now. We must bide our time and wait for an opportunity to warn the Athenians. Evil men like Hippias never win out in the end; he's sure to get caught in one of his own traps."

Alex's words calmed Stacey down a bit, though if he hadn't been holding on to her wrists very tightly, she still might have made a rush at Hippias. It was bad enough that Hippias had perverted the idea of freedom. But when he went so far as to insult Stacey's friend, Solon—well, that's when she got really mad. Still, despite the anger of his sister, Alex managed to slowly guide her back down to the sleeping quarters without Hippias or the two generals knowing that their conversation had been overheard.

✦ ✦ ✦

As Hippias had predicted, the Persian landing on the island of Euboea and their attack on the city of Eretria were complete successes for Datis and Artaphernes. The Eretrians fought nobly to defend their city, holding off the invaders for six days, but when, on the seventh, two Eretrians with an eye to their own profit betrayed the city, all hope for resistance was lost. During the darkest hour of the night, the traitors flung open the gates, and the enemy marched in. As they had done at Naxos, the Persians burnt the city and defiled its temples. Those they did not kill in the battle, they carried off as prisoners.

The next morning, the Persians once again boarded their boats and crossed the narrow strait that separated Euboea from Attica. Alex and Stacey knew that it was only a matter of a few days before Hippias would lead the Persians to Marathon, and from there to Athens. If they were going to act, they would have to act now. Alex wisely, if reluctantly, decided that the only way they could reach Athens in time was to steal a horse and ride as swiftly as they could in a southwesterly direction. His years in the Boy Scouts had taught Alex well how to tell direction using the sun and the stars, and he felt sure that once he reached the outskirts of Athens, he could find his way to the agora without much difficulty.

Accordingly, when evening fell, the children strolled casually by the corral where the war horses were kept. They had hoped to be able to sneak one of the horses out through the back, but the corral was too closely guarded to give them any hope of succeeding.

"Stacey," said Alex, "we need to find some way to distract the guards. If we can get them to leave the corral for just a few minutes, I know I can get us a horse. Look around and see if you can find something that we can use."

Stacey, who was an expert shopper and had a good eye for finding small treasures, immediately began to scan the area. In no time at all, she spied a cart on which there hung several dresses and veils worn by the dancers. About a hundred feet to the right was a second cart that housed various musical instruments.

"Alex," said Stacey, "I think I know how we can distract the guards. If you can get a hold of one of those horns over there and play a tune on it, I'll slip into one of those dresses and do a dance for the soldiers. That's sure to draw their attention away from the corral."

"Good idea, Stacey!" said Alex, and, without a second thought, he strode over to the cart and took up a large silver horn that curled around three times before it ended in a great flaring bell. Taking a deep breath, Alex began to play a fast, up-beat song that he had learned on his journey from Susa to Sardis. Stacey, meanwhile, put on one of the dresses and wrapped a veil across the bottom half of her face. In quick, light little steps she danced over to the fire and began spinning wildly on the tops of her toes.

As Alex had hoped, the moment Stacey began to dance, two things happened at once. First, all the soldiers, including the ones who were guarding the corral, gathered around Stacey and began to pound the ground with their hands and their swords. Second, all those within hearing distance who could blow a horn or beat on a drum rushed over to where Alex was playing and pulled an instrument from the cart. In no time at all, Stacey was dancing to the raucous sounds of a dozen instruments. Around and around she spun, with her arms poised perfectly in the air and her veil floating on the breeze. She was a fireball of energy. No one who looked at her could possibly look away until the dance was over. It was as if she had hypnotized everyone.

Everyone that is but Alex. Once he could see that all eyes were trained on Stacey and that there were enough musicians playing to make his own horn unnecessary, Alex slipped away and led the largest war horse out of the unguarded corral. As quietly as he could, he saddled the horse and then pulled himself up. When Stacey, who glanced at the corral every time she spun around, saw that Alex was mounted on the horse, she stopped spinning and began swaying side to side. And as she swayed, she sang:

> I'm Helen of Sparta, a Queen of the Greeks,
> But I hate all the men of my day;
> Across the Aegean my lonely heart seeks,
> O Paris, come steal me away.

When the soldiers in the audience heard the words, they all cried out their approval. Though none of them were Trojans, they were all from the East, and they applauded wildly the notion that a beautiful Greek woman would prefer a man from the East to her own fellow Greeks.

Alex waited for the applause to reach its climax, and then charged his horse directly toward Stacey. As he charged, he cried out in a loud voice, "Helen, I have come to you from across the sea." Then, leaning off the right side of the horse and stretching out his right arm, he swept his dancing sister right off her feet and deposited her safely behind him on the saddle. As the crowd roared with laughter, Alex yelled out, "Now come with me back to Troy, and forget these foolish Greeks." Again, the crowd applauded, and Alex kicked the sides of his horse as hard as he could. The horse shot forward into a fast gallop, leaving the camp, the soldiers, and the Persian army far behind.

As Alex and Stacey had hoped, the soldiers who witnessed their flight from the camp thought that it was all a show put on for their amusement, and, for that reason, they made no attempt to follow the children. Eventually, they discovered the truth, but by then Alex and Stacey were safely on their way to Athens.

Chapter
15

The Marathon Runner

When, on the following evening, Alex and Stacey reached Athens, they found that the agora was already alive with rumors of the Persian attack of Euboea. Wasting no time, Alex and Stacey dismounted and positioned themselves directly beneath the marble statues of Harmodius and Aristogeiton.

"Citizens of Athens," cried Alex, "you must listen to me. I have news of great danger to you and your city. The Persians have sacked the town of Eretria and have taken control of all Euboea.

The Gates of Freedom

They have even crossed over to Attica. Soon they will begin to move their cavalry and their foot soldiers toward the plains of Marathon. Once past there, nothing will be able to stop them from taking Athens. If you hope to save your city, you must immediately send your finest fighting men to meet the Persians at Marathon."

"Stand down, boy," said a voice in the crowd, "Who are you that we should listen to you? You are only a child."

"Look at our clothes," said Alex, "Don't you see that we are dressed as Persians. Even now we have escaped from their camp to warn you. If you still do not believe us, then let me speak words to you that will make you believe. Though the army that now moves toward Marathon is led by Datis and Artaphernes, it is being guided by an enemy who hates Athens even more than Darius: Hippias, the son of Peisistratus."

"Hippias!" shouted another voice in the crowd, "We had *heard* that he had gone over to the side of the Persians, but who would have dreamed that even he could be capable of such treachery."

"It is true, I tell you," said Alex, "Hippias has never forgiven the citizens of Athens for exiling him. He will not be satisfied till he has crushed your democracy and stolen away your freedom. My sister and I heard him say as much."

"But what chance have we against the Persians?" said a third voice, "I have heard that they sailed to Greece with a fleet of 600 ships."

"It is true," said Alex, "I do not deny it. But their ships will do them no good on the plains of Marathon. Listen to me, all of you, if you turn away from this fight, Athens will fall. And if Athens falls, then all of Greece will soon follow. It is up to you, now, to decide the fate of Greece. Either you will step aside and allow her to fall to the tyranny of Persia, or you will take up the torch and be a guiding light to all of Europe."

"But we are outnumbered," replied the third voice, "How can we hope to stand against an army that is three times our size?"

"Look above me," said Alex, "at these two statues. Did these men count numbers or weigh the cost before they struck against the tyranny of Hippias? I tell you they did not! They swore that Athens would be free even if it meant their own deaths. Each of you today has the chance to gain for himself and his family the same honor—if not greater honor—that has been accorded the memory of Harmodius and Aristogeiton. In the name of Athena, Solon, and Peisistratus, I call on you to put aside your fears and to remember that you are free men. Hippias thinks that because you are free, you are weak and care only for yourselves. But I say that with great freedom comes great responsibility; I say that you will fight harder because you are free. And you will do it, not because there is a whip at your back, but because you know that freedom is a thing worth fighting for and dying for. There was a time not long ago when I did not understand this, when I thought freedom was just a word. But I have come to see now that freedom is more than a word: it lies at the very heart of human dignity and greatness."

"Bravo, young man!" said a new voice from the back of the crowd, "You shame us with your courageous words. Here I am, one of the ten generals of Athens, and I have allowed a boy to speak words that should have come from my own lips."

"Hail, Miltiades (mill TIE a deeze)," cried a fifth voice, "You were always the bravest of the generals, as was your father before you. Lead us now into battle, and we will follow."

Immediately, a roar rose up from the crowd, and a thousand voices called in unison for Miltiades to lead them to victory at Marathon.

"Very well," said Miltiades, "I shall do as you ask. But first, let a runner be sent in all haste to Sparta. Perhaps he can convince the Spartans to join us at Marathon. Their soldiers surpass even ours in bravery and strength."

"Send me, Miltiades," said a tall, thin man with the build of an Olympic athlete.

"Ah, Pheidippides (figh DIP a deeze)," said Miltiades, "I am glad you are here. No one can match you for speed and endurance. You must leave right away for Sparta. Let them know our situation and ask them to send as many soldiers as they can to assist us at Marathon."

Without so much as a goodbye, Pheidippides dropped his outer cloak on the ground, turned on his heels, and began to run. Alex and Stacey had once seen a gazelle in a zoo, but the grace and speed of Pheidippides as he ran was a far more beautiful sight.

"Stacey," said Alex, with sudden resolve, "we *must* go with Pheidippides. He will need our help if he is to convince the Spartans."

"But Alex," replied Stacey, "that's impossible. We could never run as a fast as Pheidippides." Stacey paused for a moment and looked down at her feet. Alex could tell she was deep in thought. Suddenly, she cried out, "I have an idea!" and began running like a madwoman up the hill of the Acropolis. Alex followed after her and soon found himself standing before a wooden statue of Athena. He recognized the image at once, for it was toward this statue that the grand procession of the Panathenaea moved at the start of each festival.

The Marathon Runner

"Athena," said Stacey in a loud but sweet voice, "Hercules told us that each of us has within our veins a drop of his blood. If that is true, please do something to bring that drop of blood to life. You must have some kind of magic that can do that."

For three long, grueling minutes, nothing happened. Then, off to their left, the children heard the hoot of an owl.

"It's Athena's owl!" cried Stacey, "I'd recognize its voice anywhere. Look, Alex, it's perched on the branch of that olive tree. What's an olive tree doing up here on the Acropolis?"

"The olive tree!" said Alex, "Of course, that's the olive tree that Athena gave as a gift to the city and which convinced the Athenians to make her their patron goddess. Don't you remember? We saw it ourselves when we came to Greece three years ago. C'mon, Stacey, let's walk over to the tree, and see if the owl will perch on your shoulder."

Hand in hand, Alex and Stacey walked over to the tree, but when they got there, they realized to their dismay that the owl had disappeared. Instead, near the branch where the owl had been standing, the children saw two glowing lights. Intrigued by the lights, they pressed their faces right up against the tree. What they saw surprised them greatly. The two lights were actually two olives that shone with a warm, green glow. The children reached out their hands, and each plucked off one of the two olives. Even in their hands, they continued to glow, and it struck the children that this might be a message from Athena that they were to eat the olives. At first they were reluctant to do so, and they both tried to close their fists around the olives. But this they found they could not do. No matter how hard they concentrated, they could not close their fists. Instead, a strange magnetic force began to swirl around their hands—a force that drew their hands upward toward their faces.

Convinced now that they must eat the olives after all, they closed their eyes, threw the olives into their mouths, and bit down hard. Instantly, the children felt a bolt of electricity surge through their bodies from head to toe. Hot fingers of flame coursed along their veins and shot downward through their legs.

"Alex," shouted Stacey, "I feel like I'm on fire."

"So do I, Stacey," said Alex, "It's like the blood is boiling inside of me. I'm afraid if we don't do something fast, we both will explode."

"Yes, Alex," said Stacey, "We must *do* something, but what? We're running out of time. Another minute and I think we really *will* explode."

By now, the blood was pounding so loudly in his ears that Alex could barely hear Stacey. "Yes," he said, "we're running out of time … running out of … running … running. That's it, Stacey! We have to *run*! These olives have given us the power and energy to run as fast as Pheidippides. Follow me!"

With that, Alex swiveled around on his toes and began jumping and leaping down the rocky slope of the Acropolis as if he were a mountain goat. Stacey followed after him, and soon the two were running shoulder to shoulder. Thirty seconds later, they were racing through the agora. All around them, they heard shouts of wonder and amazement, as the crowd of people parted to let them through.

"May the gods go with you," called the voice of Miltiades behind them, "I only pray that all the citizens of Athens will show the same courage and strength."

Just as a match ignites a pile of dry wood and causes it to blaze with fire and heat, so Athena's olives had ignited the drop of Hercules's blood hidden deep inside the children's veins. Athena had done just what Stacey had asked of her; for the next several days, the children would leap and run with a speed and a force that would put swift-footed Achilles to shame.

Powered by the blood and the olives, Alex and Stacey had no problem catching up to Pheidippides. Indeed, once they had reached him, they had to slow themselves down or they would have shot right past him. For long hours, the three ran side by side in silence. The countryside was flashing by them so quickly that it made them dizzy to look at it. Besides, running along the hundred-odd miles of hills that lead from Athens to Sparta is a feat that calls for much concentration. One misstep and the runner can be sent plunging off the side of a cliff or roll down a mountainside of gritty stones and jagged rocks. The children marveled at how light Pheidippides was on his feet, as he sprang effortlessly from stone to stone. Whether he was running up a hill or down, he never lost his step, and he never slowed down.

Alex had been wondering why Miltiades had not offered them horses to ride to Sparta. Surely a horse could run faster than a man! Now that he saw how rough and hilly the terrain was between Athens and Sparta, he knew that only someone on foot could make the journey.

Normally, the children would have been exhausted after running only fifteen minutes at the pace set by Pheidippides, but with the dual magic of Hercules and Athena burning inside of them, they found that the faster they ran the *less* tired they were. Ever since he was a child, Alex had always wanted to run with the speed of a cheetah. Stacey, on the other hand, had always wanted to spring from one place to another the way a cat does. Now, the children were doing both at once. It was as if their legs were made of rubber mounted on springs. They ran and sprang without effort or fatigue, the way one only does in dreams.

On the morning of the second day they arrived, breathless but exhilarated, in the town square of Sparta. Alex and Stacey could tell at once that this was a very different city from that of Athena and Solon. Whereas Athens was decorated with graceful statues and colorful temples and was alive with merchants from all over the world, Sparta was a much rougher, cruder looking place that seemed isolated from the greater world around it. When Pheidippides and the children arrived, they were immediately escorted to an open, grassy area where a dozen gray-haired men sat spread out on a set of stone benches. Unlike the finely carved seats on which the Athenian elders sat, the Spartan benches were neither carefully sculpted nor pleasing to the eye; they merely served their purpose in a simple, practical way.

"Elders of Sparta," said Pheidippides, after he had been introduced to the members of the council, "I come to your city on urgent business. Three days ago, the Persian navy, having seized control of Euboea, landed on the northeast coast of Attica. Even as I speak, they are marching toward Marathon. Their goal is to destroy the countryside of Attica and then march directly on Athens. Thirty-six hours ago, a large Athenian force led by Miltiades left the city to meet the Persians in combat on the plains of Marathon. Spartans, I come to you now to ask your assistance in battle. All Greece rings with praises of your fighting prowess and your fearlessness on the field. We call on you to demonstrate that valor in helping us to resist the Persians."

"Pheidippides," said one of the elders, "your words move me, and I am tempted even now to take up arms myself and follow you to Athens. But that, I am afraid, is impossible. Our city is now in the midst of one of its most important festivals. None of us can leave the city until the week is out."

"But if you wait that long," broke in Alex, "it will be too late. By then the battle will be over. Athens needs your help now if she is to hold back the Persians."

"You speak boldly for one so young," said the elder, "but our traditions are sacred, and they must take precedence over the needs of other city-states."

"No!" said Alex, "that's just the point. The time is over when one city-state can ignore all the others in favor of her own selfish desires. We are not just Athenians or Spartans or Euboeans; we are Greeks! Have no rhapsodes journeyed to your city? Have you not heard the poems of Homer? Do you not know that all Greece once bonded together to fight a war against the most powerful nation in Asia? Yes, Troy fell long ago, but now a new power has risen up in the East, and it threatens to do to you what you once did to Troy. What is needed now is teamwork and a shared vision of what it means to be Greek and to be free."

"Yes, yes, boy," said the elder, "I know Homer well and am quite aware of the power of the Persian Empire, but I think you Athenians put too much store in freedom. As far as I can tell, your emphasis on freedom has caused endless bickering in your assemblies and much license and wild living among your people."

"Yes," said Alex, "freedom, like all things, can be abused by bad men. Without wisdom and temperance to keep them on track, a free people can easily go astray. But I think, as did Solon, the great founder of Athenian democracy, that the blessings of freedom outweigh the risks and the dangers. Do not you Spartans pride yourselves on your freedom to choose how you will live and in what way you will conduct your government? Believe me, if Darius were to seize control of Greece and turn her into another one of his satrapies, you would quickly lose your ability to choose such things for yourselves."

"The boy is right," said a young man who had been standing to the side of the elders, "Honor demands that we come to the aid of Athens. The gods will understand if we suspend the rules of the festival to protect the freedom of our nation."

"Patience, son of Anaxandrides (a nax an DREE deeze)," said the elder, "your own great spirit will be your undoing. You are too young to understand affairs of state."

"That may be true," said the young man, "but I am not too young to recognize excuses when I hear them! For too long, we Spartans have isolated ourselves from the rest of Greece. Here in our city we possess the strongest fighters in the world, but what good is our strength if we use it only to please ourselves. We must yield up our strength as a gift to Greece."

"Yes," said Alex, "this man is right. You must listen to what he says."

But the elder did not listen, nor did any of his fellow elders. Instead, they gave Alex, Stacey, and Pheidippides food to eat and then sent them on their way back to Athens. The children were in no mood to start running again, but Pheidippides told them that they must return to Athens as soon as possible so that they could warn the Athenian army that they would be fighting alone. After some grumbling, the children agreed, and the three runners set off. Soon, as the pace of their running increased and the wind began to whistle through their hair, the children's disappointment faded away, and they enjoyed again the thrill of their own movement.

For about five hours, Pheidippides and the children ran on in silence, until they came to the mountainous region of Tegea (TE gee ah). As the passes that ran along the sides of the mountains were steep and narrow in that part of the country, they slowed down their pace and switched to single file with Pheidippides in the lead and Alex taking up the rear. In this manner they continued on for about thirty minutes, until, without warning, Stacey suddenly found herself rushing unstoppably into the motionless back of Pheidippides. For some reason unknown to the children, Pheidippides, after rounding the bend of a particularly narrow pass, had stopped dead in his tracks.

The reason was soon made clear when, several seconds later, Stacey unglued herself from Pheidippides' back, and the children peered cautiously around the bend. There, in the middle of the pass, stood an odd little man with dark black hair. From his waist up, he looked normal enough—if one excepted the fact that his hair seemed to curl itself into two horns—but from the waist down his legs were shaped exactly like those of a goat.

Needless to say, it took the children only a moment to recognize him.

He was the king of all the satyrs (SAY ters) of Greece, and his name was Pan.

Chapter 16

The Oracle

"Pan," said Alex, after he had given him a big hug and after Stacey had taken his arms and spun with him in a circle, "what are you doing here?"

"Really, Alex," said Pan, "it is I who should be asking *you* that question. This is my home; it is you who are the strangers here."

"I guess you're right, Pan," said Alex, "It was Hercules who called us back this time. Stacey and I have been brought to Greece to help convince Leonidas the Spartan to fight the Persians at the battle of Thermopylae. But judging by the poor job we just did trying to get the Spartans to help the Athenians at Marathon, I'm not too sure we can fulfill our mission."

"Have no fear of that, young Hercules," said Pan, "You would not have been called if you did not possess the skills for your task. Besides, I have been watching you and your sister closely, and you both have performed well. But first, I must speak briefly to your companion.

"Pheidippides," said Pan, turning his attention for a moment away from the children, "you must continue on alone to Athens. The children will remain here with me. But before you go, I ask that you carry a message with you back to your fellow citizens. Tell them that for too long they have forgotten me in their prayers and rituals. They have been faithful enough in their gifts to Zeus, Athena, and Apollo, but tell them that I too have my claims. Let those who dwell in cities not forget the power and beauty of the woods and the streams. No man can live a happy and balanced life without paying his homage to Pan. Now go, and may Athena speed you on your way."

When the children had said their goodbyes to Pheidippides, and the Athenian runner had disappeared around the next bend, Pan turned back to the children and addressed them again:

"Alex and Stacey, you have been aided thus far by Hercules and Athena. It is time now that you sought the aid of another helper: the Oracle of Delphi. I know already how the blood of Hercules and the olives of Athena have gifted you with the speed of Pheidippides. Now I shall add my own magic to the mix. Here are two apples taken from the Garden of the Hesperides (he SPARE i deeze) that lies far in the western end of the world. Once you bite into them, your speed will be increased ten-fold, and you shall run faster than the hawk flies. You must run straight north until you come to the Gulf of Corinth. When you reach the edge of the water, you must leap high into the air. The magic will carry you up and over the gulf until you are caught by the magnetic pull of the omphalos (OHM fa los), the great navel stone that lies near the Temple of Apollo. It will draw you back to earth and help you to land safely at Delphi."

Alex and Stacey gave Pan another hug and then took the apples in their hands. With great excitement and not a little bit of fear, they bit into the apples. This time the effect was not so much like fire as it was like wind. Alex felt as if a tornado were forming deep in his chest and spreading itself upwards and downwards; Stacey felt as if her insides had been turned into a kite blown back and forth by a tremendous breeze. Three times, Alex and Stacey spun around like a top, then, SNAP: they shot northward as fast as an arrow from a bow. Thirty, forty, fifty miles per hour, and still their speed increased. As he ran, Alex cast a glance over at Stacey and was shocked to find that her feet were moving so quickly he could not see them. From her waist down, all he saw was a blur. They ran so fast that their feet barely touched the ground, and the leaves spun skyward as they passed. Sixty, seventy, eighty miles per hour, and still they ran faster. The landscape around them was rushing by so quickly that they could barely make out the shapes of trees and mountains. Ninety, ninety-five, one hundred! Just in time, Alex saw the water rushing toward them and screamed out to Stacey to jump.

Like two stones shot out of a catapult, Alex and Stacey soared upwards over the gulf. Instinctively, they both stretched out their arms and pointed their noses to the sky. To anyone who saw them from the ground, they would have looked like two eagles in flight. The children were afraid that their speed would soon decrease and that they would tumble down into the gulf, but this did not happen. Instead, at the very same moment that the force of their mighty jump began to ebb away behind them, an even greater force grabbed a hold of them from the front and pulled them ever higher. Soon, the water below them disappeared and was replaced by rocky hills and plains.

"Oh boy," thought Alex, "now we're in for it. If we stop moving and start to fall, we'll be smashed to bits on those rocks."

But they neither stopped nor fell. The force continued to pull them upward and forward until they suddenly stopped in mid air. With one eye closed and one eye open, the children looked below them to see a gently sloping hill. At the top was a huge stadium with an Olympic sized track. Half-way down the slope, the children spied an open-air theater that reminded them of the theater at Epidauros (e pee DOW rus) where Stacey had found the dreaming stone three years earlier. Finally, below that, they saw a great temple that reminded them of the Parthenon in Athens.

"I recognize this place," said Alex, "It's Delphi, the home of the Oracle. That's the Temple of Apollo below us"

Even as Alex spoke these words, the children began sinking slowly toward the temple as though they were riding on an invisible elevator. For one long, lovely minute they felt exactly like two feathers gliding gracefully on a pocket of air. When their feet finally touched the ground, they found that they were standing on an odd-shaped rock that looked like it had been dug from a secret cavern deep in the earth.

"That must be the omphalos Pan told us about," said Stacey, "It gives me an eerie feeling just to look at it. I wonder why Pan called it a navel stone; it doesn't look like a belly button."

"It is called the omphalos because it was cast up to us from the navel of the earth," said a strong female voice behind them, "As the navel of a man lies at the mid-point of his body, so this stone was formed in the very center of the earth; as it is through his navel that a child is first nourished in the belly of his mother, so does the omphalos draw in to it all the energy of the universe. You stand, children, at the nexus, the crossroad of all that has come or will come."

Alex and Stacey turned quickly to see the figure of a tall, thin woman dressed in a flowing robe made from a single unbroken piece of coal black cloth. They knew at once who she was.

"Yes, children," she said, "I am the Oracle of Delphi. I have long awaited your coming, for your journey here and the mission behind it are also a nexus, a crossroad in the history of the world. I see by your faces that you are worried, but there is no need. The battle at Marathon is going well. If you wish to see it, simply gaze deep into the heart of the omphalos."

Alex and Stacey did as she asked, and soon, strange patterns of light and dark began to dance in crisscrossing lines over the stone. The children sharpened their gaze, and the lines began to form into the image of a long field of grass. Over the grass, the dark figures of horses galloped swiftly by with armed men clutching tightly to their backs. Next, two divisions of soldiers rushed toward each other on the grassy field, their swords extended and their shields held high. The children could tell by the soldiers' uniforms which were the Greeks and which were the Persians. They even spotted Miltiades himself calling out to his troops to charge at the enemy. At first, the men seemed afraid to look at the Persians, but Miltiades called to them again, and this time they looked the Persians dead in the eye. The Athenian charge caused panic among the Persian troops and many of them scattered and broke their lines.

All of this seemed to be occurring at the far right of the battlefield. In the center of the battle, the Persians held their lines and pushed forward. This concerned Alex greatly, but as he cast his eye further down to the left of the field, he saw that here too the Persian line was breaking. "Yes," thought Alex to himself, "I see now what Miltiades is up to. He will first break through the right and left wing of the Persian forces where their weaker soldiers are stationed, and then turn inward to crush the stronger fighters from three different points at once." Even as Alex thought these things, they materialized magically in the center of the omphalos. By the end of the day, the Athenians had crushed the Persian assault. Everywhere, the bodies of Persian soldiers lay scattered in the dust. Here and there, Alex saw Greek bodies as well, but they were vastly outnumbered by the piles of Persian corpses that lay rotting in the late afternoon sun.

"They've done it, Stacey," said Alex, "Even without the Spartans, the Athenians have won the day. I hope that teaches Darius a lesson about the courage of free men."

"Children," said the Oracle, "I think you've had enough excitement for one day. Come into the temple and let us have supper together. I have many things to ask you about your journeys. My spirit tells me that this is not the first time you have come to ancient Greece."

For the next several hours, the children devoted themselves to eating and drinking and to answering the endless questions of the Oracle. Before they knew it, it was night, and the constellations huddled above them as though drawn together by the omphalos. But no one felt like going to bed. They had too many stories to share.

The Oracle

Finally, as the hour approached midnight, the Oracle told the children that they had best get some sleep.

Stacey yawned and said, "Yes, I really am sleepy. It seems like all we've been doing for the last three days is rushing from one place to the next. First we rush out of the Persian camp to warn Athens about Marathon, then we rush out of Athens to try to get help from the Spartans, and now we've rushed out of Sparta to come here to Delphi."

"So," said a voice in the darkness, "it is you two who warned the Athenians. I promise you that you will pay for your treachery!"

Though the night had been a calm one thus far, the moment the stranger spoke, a bolt of lightning cut through the sky and lit up the area around the temple. It was a brief flash, but it was long enough for both of the children to recognize the face of the man who had spoken.

It was the face of Hippias.

❖ ❖ ❖

Being at heart a coward, Hippias ran from the battlefield of Marathon as soon as he realized that the victory would go to Athens. He was quite a good horseman, and he had been riding steadily all day. Though most of his plans had been crushed by the Persian defeat, he had hoped that the Oracle might reveal to him a different strategy for taking back Athens.

He had just arrived at Delphi when he overheard Stacey reveal the part she had played in warning Athens of the invasion. Feeling assured that there were no guards or even priests to stop him, Hippias rushed forward at the children and grabbed a hold of Stacey. He dragged her outside the temple and pressed a dagger to her throat.

"Listen to me Oracle," he said slowly, "I have come here with a question for you. Answer me well, and this child may yet live."

"Ask your question, evil man," said the Oracle.

"Last night I dreamed that I slept in my mother's bed. Since my mother is Athens, then the bed must be Greece. Tell me, Oracle, does this dream mean that I will yet conquer Greece?"

As Hippias awaited his answer, Stacey tried her best to break free of his grasp. Her attempt failed, but it caused the top of her hair to brush against Hippias' nose. The movement tickled him, and before he could stop himself, Hippias broke into a fit of uncontrollable sneezing. The sneezing had two important effects. First, it caused Hippias to break his hold and gave Stacey the chance to slip away unharmed. Second, as Hippias was an old man, and as the men of his day had little training in proper dental care, the force of the sneeze caused one of his teeth to fly right out of his mouth. Hippias fell to his knees and tried to recover the tooth, but no matter how hard he searched, he could not find it.

"Ha ha!" cried Alex, "now I see the meaning of your dream. The only part of Greece that you shall ever own, tyrant, is the piece of earth that now holds your tooth."

"May Zeus strike me dead," roared Hippias, "if you and your sister are still alive when the sun rises. I may have lost Athens, but you will lose far more."

Hippias made a lunge toward Alex and Stacey, but this time they were ready for him. Before they had landed on the omphalos, Alex had gotten a very good bird's-eye view of the slope of Delphi, and so he knew just where to run. Grabbing his sister's hand, Alex rushed through the back of the temple and began climbing the slope toward the theater. Once they reached the stage, Alex bent over and scooped up a handful of sharp stones. He dumped the stones into Stacey's hands and then bent down to get more for himself. Then, he instructed Stacey to run up the right side of the rows of seats, while he ran up the left. There they waited until Hippias, torn and bleeding from trying to make his way up in the dark, appeared on the stage below. Seconds later, another bolt of lightning lit up the sky and fell on the miserable Hippias like a spotlight.

"Now, Stacey," shouted Alex, and the two children began to pelt the hapless Hippias with their stones. With nothing to protect him from the rain of stones, Hippias fell to the ground and covered his head with his hands. But even this afforded him little protection. The rocks cut into his flesh, leaving him weak and bruised.

"C'mon, Stacey," said Alex, "follow me. There's a winding path that leads up to the stadium. I'm sure I can find it."

Alex found it alright, but the path was even steeper than he had expected. It left the children feeling winded and light headed, but their pains were nothing compared to those of Hippias. Such was his rage that he followed the children up the path, even though he knew his heart could hardly bear the strain of the steep ascent. Higher and higher the children climbed, as their relentless pursuer followed them up the path.

After what seemed like hours, Hippias managed to drag his beaten body into the stadium. Unfortunately for him, his success proved a bitter one. Just as they had done before in the theater, Alex and Stacey stood poised on one of the rows of steep seats that circled the stadium. For the third time, a bolt of lightning, as if sent by Zeus himself, crashed over head, revealing the position of the evil son of Peisistratus. As soon as they saw him, the children let loose a second volley of stones. The blow knocked Hippias to the ground and bruised his back and head.

"Your days are numbered, Hippias," shouted Alex, "Greece will have no more tyrants in her land. The time of freedom is at hand."

"I will kill you yet," cried Hippias.

"With what?" answered Alex, "I see no sword or dagger in your hand."

"Here is my sword!" replied Hippias. In one swift, graceful movement, Hippias rose to his feet, drew a long metal blade from the sheath at his side, and held it aloft for Alex to see.

That, of course, was exactly what Alex had hoped he would do. As Hippias swung his sword wildly, a fourth and final bolt of lightning cut its way through the still night air and struck the sword. For a moment, the body of Hippias seemed frozen in mid-air—as straight and as rigid as the statues of Harmodius and Aristogeiton. Then, with a thud that shook the stadium above and the temple below, the body of Hippias fell to the earth. As Alex and Stacey looked on with horror, the ground beneath Hippias cracked open to form a dark yawning mouth that sucked the body down into the heart of the mountain.

"A fitting end," said Alex gravely, "for one who thought the earth belonged to him." Then, taking Stacey's hand in his, he led her slowly back down the mountain to the temple. There the Oracle met them and led them further down to a hidden cavern where she had prepared two beds of finely wrought silver.

With two groans of satisfaction, Alex and Stacey lay down on the beds and instantly fell into a deep sleep. Over their heads, the Oracle sang a haunting melody.

Chapter

17

An Unlikely Savior

When Alex and Stacey awoke the next morning, they felt more refreshed and alive than they had ever felt before.

"Alex," said Stacey, "I can't believe it. I feel like we've been sleeping for months and months. Maybe even years and years."

"That's strange," said Alex, "I feel the same way. It's like … like I've been suspended in a pool of water … but the water wasn't water … it was more like … like … time."

"You speak wisely," said the Oracle, who had entered silently into the chamber where Alex and Stacey had been sleeping, "You have indeed been suspended in time. While you were sleeping your dreamless sleep, nine years have come and gone on the earth. Men have died, women have given birth, and a new king has risen in Persia."

"A new king?" said Alex, "You must be referring to Xerxes."

"Exactly," said the Oracle, "Four years after his assault on Greece, Darius died and was succeeded by Xerxes, his son by the daughter of Cyrus. For the last five years, Xerxes has concentrated his efforts on securing his holdings in Egypt. But now that he has crushed the rebels of the south, he turns his eye west toward Greece. He has at his side a Greek advisor as cunning and prideful as Hippias. This time, however, the Greek traitor is an exiled king of Sparta who would use the Persians to gain his own selfish revenge. His name is Demaratus (de ma RA tus), and he holds the ear of Xerxes as Hippias did that of Darius."

"How can freedom and democracy survive," said Alex, "when she has as many enemies inside as outside?"

"You speak truly," said the Oracle, "Not all who are raised in free cities are free in their minds. Many there are who despise the people and would take unto themselves the power to speak and think for their fellow citizens. The only thing they understand is force."

"But what about Athens?" said Stacey, "Has she been able to keep her democracy safe from people like that?"

"Children," said the Oracle, "these last nine years have been difficult ones for Athens, filled with much conflict and strife between those who would expand the reforms of Solon and those who would make Athens into another Sparta. Still, out of this turmoil, there has arisen one who has the potential to save all Greece. His name is Themistocles (tha MIST oh cleeze), and he combines within himself the wisdom of Solon and the cunning

An Unlikely Savior

of Peisistratus. He is, to tell the truth, a most unlikely savior. His mother was not an Athenian—some say she was not even a Greek—and his family was neither wealthy nor of ancient blood. He is by nature rash, impetuous, and unscrupulous, yet there burns within him a deep-seated nobility and a love for Athens, her people, and her democracy. But I needn't tell you any more, for you will soon meet him face to face."

"Oracle," said Alex, "are you sending us back to Athens?"

"No," she said, "you need not leave this temple to meet the great Themistocles. In fact, I anticipate his arrival at any moment."

"He's coming *here*?" said Stacey, "But why?"

"Why does anyone travel to Delphi?" asked the Oracle, "They travel here that they may learn what the future has in store. They come that their fears might be soothed and their riddles solved. Earlier this year, when Athens heard that Persia was building up once more for war, she sent a deputation to Delphi to ask a single question: can we defeat the Persians in battle or should we surrender? I took their question to the god, and in reply I was told that Athens' only hope for survival would come from her wooden walls."

"Her wooden walls?" said Stacey, "But what does it mean?"

"I do not know," said the Oracle.

"What do you mean, you don't know?" said Alex sharply, "I thought you were the Oracle."

"I am only a pipe," said the Oracle, "through which the god blows his spirit. You might as well ask the horn the name of the song that the musician plays, or ask the pen to explain the meaning of the drama the poet writes. I have spoken many prophecies in my life, but there are very few that I have fully understood. The future is dark, and the ways of the gods are strange."

For several minutes, no one spoke. The Oracle seemed to fall into a deep trance, and the children withdrew into their own private thoughts. Alex remembered what his father had told him long ago: that the difference between mythology and the Bible was that the first was like a candle and the second like the sun. Stacey, meanwhile, tried to recall a verse she had once memorized for Sunday school: something about seeing things dimly in a mirror. The air in the room grew thick and heavy, and the children felt as though there were a presence in the room.

"Enough!" said the Oracle, breaking the children out of their separate reveries, "The hour has come. Your savior has arrived."

❖ ❖ ❖

Themistocles was everything the Oracle had said he would be. The man seemed incapable of standing still. Even as he spoke with the Oracle, he would leap up from his seat, pace the room nervously, and wring his hands. One got dizzy just watching him. Again and again, he tried to get the Oracle to give him a clear answer as to what the "wooden walls" were, but her only reply was silence.

"There are many in Athens," said Themistocles, "who believe that the wooden walls refer to the Acropolis, which used to be circled by a thick fence. They say that the only thing we can do is to barricade ourselves in the Acropolis and wait there for the Persians. Others say they refer to a partial wall that has been built from Athens down to the port of Piraeus (pie RAY us); they would have us secure these walls so we can keep supplies flowing from the port to the city. But I am not satisfied with either of these interpretations.

"Besides that, we have another problem in Athens. Over the past year, we found a rich new vein of silver in our mines that has filled the public treasury with a windfall of new money. Many on the council want to divide up this money and give it to the citizens, but I believe we should use the money to build up our army so that we will be ready when the Persians invade. There are too many in Athens today who have come to think, as do the Spartans, that our city is the only one in Greece. I have tried to convince them to think of all Greece as a single city, but they do not listen."

"In our country," said Alex, "we have a saying: united we stand; divided we fall."

"Exactly!" said Themistocles, "that is what I have tried to teach them. I told them that we might even have to abandon our city to the Persians if that were the only way to win the war. The question is not, how can we save this city or that city from destruction, but how can we save Greece from becoming enslaved to Persia. If we are going to call on the rest of Greece to sacrifice for this war, then we in Athens must be willing to sacrifice as well."

"Themistocles," said Alex, "why don't you hold the Persians back at Thermopylae?"

"Thermopylae?" said Themistocles, "Yes, that's a good idea. But that will only help us against the Persian army. What about their navy? They are sure to send both this time, and in larger numbers than they did before. Our navy is not strong enough to hold back the full might of the Persian fleet."

"Then," said Alex, "you must use the extra money you mentioned to build a fleet of ships. The Spartans already have an invincible army. If you can convince them to hold the pass at Thermopylae, then Athens can use her new fleet to fight the Persian navy. With Sparta on land and Athens on the sea, you just might be able to defeat Xerxes."

"Oracle," said Themistocles, "who are these children? They speak with the wisdom of Apollo himself. As soon as I return to Athens, I shall do all in my power to convince the council to use the money from the silver mines to build a hundred battleships. The Athenians have always been great sailors, and our city boasts the best shipbuilders in Europe. Not far from Athens is a forest with trees of the finest wood. We shall set our axes to those trees and build from them a navy that shall rival that of Persia herself."

"That's it, Themistocles," said Stacey, "You've solved the riddle."

"What do you mean, my girl?" said Themistocles, "What riddle have I solved?"

"The wooden walls," said Stacey, "the wooden walls. It's not the walls around the Acropolis that will save Athens but the fleet of ships that you will build. Just think of it. A hundred wooden ships side by side; what better wall could there be to hold back an invasion."

"Athena be praised," said Themistocles, "You children are a godsend. I can't wait to get back to Athens. It's sure to be a long fight, but I will not rest until I've convinced all of Athens to follow the course we have laid out today. Then, once I have done that, I will have to travel to Sparta and convince *their* citizens that they must join us in a combined resistance. I only hope they will agree to our plan."

"Themistocles," said Alex, "we've met the Spartans, and they are a proud and suspicious people. I can't imagine that they will agree to serve under Athenian commanders."

"You're right," said Themistocles, "that will be a problem. Well, it is Athens then who will have to lay down her pride and let Spartan commanders give the orders. All that matters now is that Greece survive the war that is to come. Thank you children for your help, and thank you Oracle for agreeing to see me. When this crisis is over, and if Greece is still standing, I shall dedicate a dozen gold tripods to your temple. Now farewell, and pray the Athenians will heed my words."

Themistocles leapt back on to his horse and disappeared in a cloud of dust

"Well," said the Oracle, "what did I tell you? A most unlikely savior indeed!"

Chapter 18

In the Court of Xerxes

After consuming a breakfast of truly Homeric proportions—a nine-year sleep is a marvelous way to build up an appetite!—Alex turned to the Oracle and asked her the question that had been burning in his mind all morning:

"What now, Oracle? Where do we go from here?"

"Back to Persia, of course," said the Oracle.

"Persia!" groaned Alex and Stacey together, "Not again!"

"I'm afraid you have no other choice," said the Oracle, "The time has come when you must meet the great enemy. If you are to convince Leonidas to stand up to Xerxes and his army, then you must learn what type of a man Xerxes is."

"Xerxes, Xerxes," said Stacey, "Every time I hear that name it sounds so familiar to me. I'm sure that I've heard it before, but I can't remember where."

"Yes, Stacey," said Alex, "I feel the same way. But none of that matters right now. What I want to know is how we can possibly get back to Persia? I don't suppose you have a magic fruit that can make us run over the water?"

"No, my friend," laughed the Oracle, "I know of no such fruit. But you are forgetting about the omphalos. Its powers are great; even I have not tapped all of them. Perhaps if you and your sister sit on top of it and hold hands ..."

"No way!" cut in Alex, "I know what you're thinking, and I just won't stand for it! I can just see it. The moment we sit on that omphalos it will start spinning, and I *hate* spinning rides."

"C'mon, Alex," said Stacey, "it will be fun."

"No, Stacey," said Alex, "and that's final! Since we left the Alamo, who knows how long ago, I've been spun in every direction. *No more spinning!*"

"Relax, my boy," said the Oracle, "I promise you that there will be no spinning this time. Directly under this temple lie a series of caverns that no one has ever explored. In fact all of Delphi sits upon a great fold in the earth, what the people of your day call a fault line. Many times I have felt the earth tremble beneath me. Why do you think Delphi is such a sacred place? It is because all the lines and cracks of that hidden world beneath our feet converge at this point. Delphi is like the omphalos itself—a nexus or crossroad of converging energies. Now please, children, sit on the stone and hold each other's hands."

The children did as she asked, and the Oracle spoke a spell that caused them to stick to the stone as though it were made of glue. "All is ready," she said, "Hold on tightly to each other. There will be no spinning, but there *will* be a long drop."

"What!" said Stacey, "I hate big drops almost as much as Alex hates spinning rides."

But it was too late. With a mighty crack, the ground beneath them ripped open, and they plunged downward into the belly of the earth. As they descended, the Oracle heard two distinct sounds: Stacey screaming, and Alex laughing.

After a fall of nearly three-hundred feet, the omphalos shot forward through a narrow cavern. It made the children think of the shaft they had crawled through in the palace of Darius, when the Magi had rescued them from their locked room. The only difference was that instead of crawling at a pace of one foot per minute, they were now soaring at a speed of over two-hundred miles per hour. It was a wild ride, indeed. The cavern was anything but straight, and the omphalos darted constantly back and forth to avoid smashing into a wall. When the first cavern ended, the omphalos simply shifted into another, and then another.

The summer before, the children had visited an amusement park that featured an in-the-dark roller coaster. Their ride on the omphalos was similar to that, except that *this* roller coaster moved fifty times faster and had a thousand more turns. As it was pitch black in the caverns, the children never knew when the omphalos would shift to the right or to the left, or suddenly plunge downward for another hundred feet. They just held on and prayed they wouldn't fall into a bottomless pit or be dashed against the side of a cavern.

Finally, after what felt like hours, the omphalos came to a sudden stop and began, slowly, to ascend toward the surface. Alex and Stacey expected to be greeted by a sudden burst of air and light, but instead, they found themselves in a pool of water. Afraid they might drown, Alex grabbed a hold of Stacey's shirt and kicked upward. It only took a moment before their heads popped up out of the water. It took several more seconds before they realized exactly where they were. They were standing in the fountain of Poseidon that lay at the center of the enclosed garden in the royal palace at Susa.

✦ ✦ ✦

"What great magic is this," said a booming voice, "that produces children out of water? Remove them at once from my royal fountain and bring them before me."

Four powerful arms grabbed the shoulders of Alex and Stacey and pulled the wet children out of the fountain. Then, their feet never touching the ground, they were carried with great haste before a man who sat on an ivory throne.

"Lord Xerxes," said the guard who was holding Alex, "here are the children. What shall we do with them?"

"Put them down and leave my presence," said Xerxes.

The guards did as they were told, and Xerxes turned his burning gaze upon the children: "Who are you, and by what power have you been transported into my garden?"

Figuring that what had worked for Darius would also work for Xerxes—and figuring as well that it was now the truth—Alex stood up and boldly said: "Lord Xerxes, we have been sent by the Oracle of Delphi."

"Strange!" said Xerxes, "my father Darius once told me that on the eve of his expedition to Greece he too met two children sent by the Oracle. Let us hope that you do not bring me the same bad fortune that befell my father. But do not fear! Today, I am in a mood to be gracious to all who visit my court, no matter their means of entry. If you look around, you will see that my garden is decorated for a great banquet. For seven days I have feasted with my nobles and allowed them to partake of my finest wines. Tonight you may join us. Feel free to walk about the garden."

Alex and Stacey accepted Xerxes' invitation and found to their surprise that the enclosed garden of Xerxes was, if possible, three times more beautiful than that of Darius. Marble pillars had been erected throughout the courtyard, each pillar adorned with a set of silver rings. Through the rings, silks and satins of every color had been strung like lights on a Christmas tree. It was like being in a fairyland. If it were possible, Stacey would have been happy to live in that garden all her life. Soon, the guests began to arrive, and the sounds of joy and laughter rang through the courtyard and echoed in the palace halls.

"Friends," said Xerxes, in a voice that suggested he had been drinking much wine, "I welcome you to the final night of my banquet. Tomorrow, I set out with my troops to conquer Greece, for the glory of my father and the glory of Persia. I take with me the largest army and navy that have ever been assembled in the history of the world. I will teach those rebellious barbarians what it means to sit in the shadow of my disfavor. For too long their claims to be free and independent have offended my ears and those of my father. Soon they will learn how little their precious freedom is worth when they become subject to the might of Persia. It is the way of things that only one shall rule and all the rest obey.

"But let us forget such matters for now. For this last night we shall give ourselves over to drink and revelry. Ho, guard, go and fetch Vashti (VASH tee), my Queen. I would that she would display her beauty for my guests."

The guard left immediately through the south gate, only to return several minutes later with a look of fear on his face.

"Guard," said Xerxes, "why does your face hang so? You know that I forbid anyone, on pain of death, to come into my presence with a sorrowful look. Where is my Queen?"

"Forgive me, Lord Xerxes," said the guard, changing the expression of his face to look less mournful, "but Queen Vashti refuses to come. It is for that reason my face looked sad."

"What?" roared Xerxes, dashing his goblet to the ground, "return at once to Vashti and tell her that from this very hour she is no longer my Queen or my wife. She is to be cast out on to the streets. When I return from Greece, I shall choose another Queen, one who knows how to obey her master."

Xerxes' anger put a bit of a damper on the banquet, but after an hour or so, and several more glasses of wine, the guests began to laugh again, and even Xerxes took part in the renewed festivities. As for Alex and Stacey, they decided that they did not much like this Xerxes. Where Darius had been cold and calculating, Xerxes was wild and impulsive. He could just as well hug you as stab you in the back. He would be a difficult and unpredictable enemy for the Greeks to defeat.

Eventually, after several more hours of drinking and laughter, the guests slowly began to file out of the courtyard and up to their sleeping chambers in the palace. An hour more, and Alex and Stacey discovered, to their great relief, that they were alone in the garden. To try to take their minds off all they had seen and heard, they began strolling casually among the fountains and columns, stopping now and then to smell the fragrances that dripped from the exotic flowers.

"Look, Alex," said Stacey, as they passed a small fountain near the east gate, "the figure on this fountain looks just like Hercules. You can even see the club in his hand and the lion skin draped over his head."

"You're right, Stacey," said Alex, "The sculptor must have been a genius. The statue looks so life-like that I wouldn't be surprised if it stepped right out of the fountain."

"Then *be* surprised, my fine young orator," said the statue, and promptly stepped out onto the marble walkway that circled the fountain.

"Hercules!" cried Alex and Stacey together.

"Yes," said Hercules, "it is I. I have come here to tell Alex that the time is drawing near when he will meet Leonidas face to face. But first, he must journey with the army of Xerxes as they march from Asia to Europe. North of Delphi and Thermopylae, lies a region of Greece known as Thessaly (THESS a lee); north of that, lies yet another region known as Macedonia (ma si DOE nee ah). If a traveler were to journey to Macedonia and then turn due east, he would come upon the lands of Thrace. Were he then to cross Thrace and turn south again, it would lead him down along the coast of Ionia. But there would be one obstacle. Between the southern tail of Thrace and the northern ear of the Ionian Coast there runs a narrow strait of water called the Hellespont. In his mad desire to conquer Greece, Xerxes plans to use a thousand ships to bridge the opposite shores of the Hellespont. Such is his madness that he would turn the sea into land and make Asia and Europe into a single continent.

"Alex, you must cross this bridge with Xerxes and follow his army across Thrace and down through the lands of Macedonia and Thessaly. Once you have done that, you will come in sight of the pass at Thermopylae. From there you must escape and make your way to the Spartan camp of Leonidas."

"Hey," said Stacey, "wait a minute! Why do you keep talking about Alex, but say nothing about me? You speak as if Alex were going to do this all by himself? Don't I get to help?"

"Daughter," said Hercules, "your brother *will* be going alone. For you, I have a different task, one no less dangerous and no less vital."

"You mean," said Stacey with a look of fear on her face, "that you are splitting us up?"

"Yes," said Hercules, "I am afraid that I must. It is not only the lands and freedom of Greece that lie threatened by the tyranny of Xerxes. When he returns two years from now to Susa, an incident will occur that will make him the enemy as well of that other nation whose laws and beliefs lie at the very heart of the freedom that your world takes for granted."

"You mean the Jews, don't you?" said Stacey, "Our Daddy has told us many times that the foundations set by the Greeks and the Jews are what helped to make our country and our people what they are."

"Yes, daughter," said Hercules, "it will be your task to help the Jews, as it will be your brother's to help the Greeks. Should either the Jewish or Greek nations cease to exist or lose their sense of their own unique identity, the future as you know it will never be born."

"I'm not afraid, Hercules," said Stacey, "I know I would not have been chosen for this task if I did not have the skills to complete it."

"Now," said Hercules, "you speak like the true princess that you are! While your brother accompanies Xerxes to Greece and meets with Leonidas at Thermopylae, you will be sent ahead two years to greet Xerxes when he returns from battle. Shortly after his return, he will make a search for a new queen to replace Vashti. The one he chooses will be of Jewish blood, and her name will be Esther."

"Esther!" said Stacey with great excitement, "Now I know why the name Xerxes sounded so familiar. Three years ago, our children's choir at church put on a musical about Esther. I know the whole story."

"It is well that you do," said Hercules, "Perhaps your knowledge will help you to inspire Esther to rescue her people from Xerxes, even as your brother's knowledge will help him to inspire Leonidas to rescue his. Know ye this, my hero and my princess: the gods made man and woman, and at the center of their hearts they placed a single defining virtue. For man, that virtue is courage; for woman, that virtue is beauty! But know this as well: that within true courage there lies a seed of beauty, and within true beauty there lies a seed of courage. If you two can help Leonidas and Esther to find those virtues within themselves, then you will have succeeded in your double mission.

"Now, my fellow freedom-fighters, it is time for you to say your farewells. When you are done, I shall take Stacey with me into the future, and leave you here Alex to sleep by the side of my fountain."

Neither Alex nor Stacey really liked the idea of being separated, but they weren't going to let themselves appear weak before Hercules. And so, holding back their tears, the two siblings gave each other a tight hug and two kisses on each cheek.

"Be careful, Stacey," said Alex, "I don't know what I would do without you."

"Don't worry, Alex," said Stacey, "I'll be alright. But do try to think about me when you get the chance."

"I will, Stacey," said Alex, "I promise."

Stacey gave Alex one last longing look as she reached out her hand to Hercules. Then, with silent step and slow, she walked across the garden until sister could no longer see brother, and brother could no longer see sister.

— Part —
3

Male And Female

*… who knoweth whether thou art
come to the kingdom for such a time as this?*
—Esther 4:14

Chapter 19

On the Road to War

When Alex awoke the next morning, he half-expected Stacey to still be there beside him. "Perhaps," he thought to himself as he lay with his eyes still closed, "it was all a dream. Maybe Hercules was never here in the garden at all; it was just seeing his statue that made us think of him." But alas, when he had finally mustered the courage to open his eyes and look around him, he quickly discovered that it had not been a dream. Stacey was gone, and he was alone.

The realization did not exactly make him feel afraid—at least not the kind of fear one feels in the presence of physical danger—but it made him feel more lonely than he had ever felt before. Through every phase of their journey, even when she had been silent, Stacey had been there. Indeed, for as long he could remember, Stacey had *always* been there. Oh, there had been times, *many* times, when she had driven him nearly crazy with her teasing and her silly games. But then again, she could always make him laugh, no matter how sad or angry he felt. She had a special zany kind of quality that lit up the room around her. Alex knew that he would miss that, that the world would seem just a little less colorful without her there.

"Well, Hercules," he said out loud, as he reached out his hand and touched the side of the statue, "there's no use worrying about it. You've given me a job, and it's my duty to finish that job no matter what it takes. Heck, if I can't convince Leonidas to stand firm at Thermopylae, then there might never have been a Texas for Stacey and I to grow up in."

"To whom are you speaking?" said a voice behind him, "Do you have the power to converse with statues? And where is the girl who was with you last night?"

Alex turned to see the suspicious face of Xerxes looking down at him. "Your majesty," said Alex in his most innocent voice, "my sister has returned to the Oracle, but I have remained behind to accompany you on your expedition to Greece. My name is Alex."

Xerxes thought deeply for a moment, and then replied, "Very well, boy, I shall grant your request to accompany me. But see to it that you obey my orders and that you do not attempt any treachery. I will be watching you closely, as will my advisors. You may be surprised to know that one of my closest advisors is a former Greek king."

On the Road to War

"I am well aware," said Alex, "that Demaratus the Spartan holds your ear, and that he hopes someday to rule Sparta in the name of the Persian Empire."

"Ah," said Xerxes, "I see that you are indeed a disciple of the Oracle and that she has shared with you some of her wisdom. It is very true that Demaratus has my ear and that I have promised him a throne in Sparta. But what of it? From what I have heard, the Spartans are more like us than they are like those accursed Athenians. The Spartans know what discipline means and speak little of freedom and democracy."

"In that, O king, you are both correct and mistaken. I have met the Spartans, and it is true that they know less of freedom than do the Athenians. Still, I do not think that the Spartans will so easily turn control of their nation over to Persia. They are a proud and strong people not used to taking orders from non-Spartans. You shall be resisted, O king."

"That remains to be seen, boy," said Xerxes, "When the Greeks see the size and power of my army and navy, they will throw down their weapons and beg for their lives. I propose to march my army across Thrace and down through Macedonia into Greece; as we march on land, my fleet will follow our course along the coast. No one will be able to stop us."

"Beware, my Lord," said Alex, "In Greece we say that hubris (HUGH briss) goes just before a fall. Hubris means pride: excessive, overbearing pride. Many a man and nation have been destroyed by it."

"Don't preach to me, boy," said Xerxes with anger in his voice, "I have had dreams and visions in which I see all Europe and Asia united under my crown. It is my destiny to rule the world from my throne here in Susa."

"Did not your royal father, Darius, tell you of how Solon taught both Croesus and Cyrus to look to the end and to count no man lucky until his death?"

"Of course he told me that tale," said Xerxes, "but I am no child to be frightened by bedtime stories."

"Did he tell you, then, of Polycrates (poe LI kra teeze), the great tyrant of the island of Samos (SAH mohs)? He, like you, O king, was rich and powerful, with a mighty army to protect him. He once boasted of his success to a wise man of Egypt, but the Egyptian told him to beware of his success. 'The gods,' said the Egyptian, 'often punish men who are too lucky. Therefore, I say to you that you must immediately take your most precious possession and throw it away. Then perhaps you will avoid the envy of the gods and of men.'

"Polycrates thought this good advice, and so he gathered six of his best men and rowed with them far out into the Aegean. Once there, Polycrates removed from his finger a priceless ring which he loved dearly, and tossed it into the sea. One week later, as Polycrates prepared for dinner, a poor fisherman knocked on the door of the palace. 'My lord,' he said, 'while fishing today I caught a marvelous fish of great size. I thought the fish too good for my poor table, and so I have brought it to you as a gift.' Polycrates paid the man handsomely and ordered his cooks to prepare the fish for his dinner. When the meal had been prepared, Polycrates cut into the fish and found there, in its belly, the ring he had thrown into the sea.

"Immediately, he wrote a letter to the wise man in Egypt to ask him the meaning of these strange affairs. 'Surely,' he thought, 'this must mean good fortune for me and my kingdom.' But the Egyptian replied that the very opposite was true. Nothing now could prevent Polycrates' doom. As I'm sure you yourself know,

O Xerxes, Polycrates met a terrible fate indeed. Though he was warned by prophets and by his own daughter to be wary of certain men who claimed to be his allies, Polycrates dismissed their advice. In the end, he was betrayed, killed, and his body left to hang on a cross.

"My own father told me this story, O Xerxes, and I think it best that you remember it as well. Abandon your mad desire to unite Asia and Europe. I know that you plan to bridge the Hellespont. If you do, I fear that the gods will visit their wrath upon you."

At this, Alex could see that Xerxes was considerably nettled, and for a moment, he thought that Xerxes might really take his advice and call off his attack on Greece. But Xerxes was too proud and hotheaded to take such advice.

"Enough fables, boy," he said, "I am a man of action and put little stock in stories. My army leaves within the hour. I suggest you prepare yourself. The journey will be a long and difficult one with few pleasures along the way."

With that, Xerxes stormed out of the garden and began barking orders to his servants. There was no stopping him or his expedition. Greece would soon feel the wrath of his anger.

✦ ✦ ✦

In one respect, Xerxes was wrong. There was much pleasure to be had as his troops marched along the royal road from Susa to Sardis. In fact, the best moment of all took place several days before they reached Sardis. Shortly after crossing the river Halys into the region of Lydia, they were met by a rich man named Pythius (PITH ee us) who invited Xerxes and his entire army to stay with him and enjoy his hospitality. Pythius proved a gracious host, and the troops ate and drank until their bellies seemed fit to burst. When the meal was over, Pythius rose, took the hand of Xerxes, and pledged not only to give his troops great stores of food to take with them on their march but a chest full of gold to help pay for Xerxes' expedition.

"Pythius," said Xerxes, "since I left Susa, no other rich man has shown me such hospitality. In honor of your generosity, I offer you my personal friendship and pledge to give you twice as much gold as you gave us when I return from Greece. I will also grant you now whatever request you ask of me."

"Your majesty is too kind," said Pythius, "What more can I ask of you than your friendship? You honor my house with your presence."

So spoke Pythius and moved the heart of Xerxes to laughter and joy. But the following morning, as the army prepared to resume its march, Pythius ran over to Xerxes and spoke:

"O king, last night you promised to grant me anything I asked. If you mean this truly, then there is a small favor I would ask of you. I have five sons, all of whom are serving now in your army. Lord Xerxes, I am an old man, and I do not know how long I will live. I ask that you allow but one of my five sons—the eldest—to remain behind with me and manage my affairs. The other four I give you gladly."

Then it was that Alex saw the evil and hatred of which the rash Xerxes was capable. No sooner had Pythius spoken these words than Xerxes' face flushed red, and his eyes filled with fire. "You ungrateful dog," he cried, "I myself am going on this expedition. I will be risking my own life on the fortunes of war. And now you tell me that you would keep one of your sons at home, as though his life were of more value than mine. Since I gave you my pledge, I will grant your request, but I do not think it will prove to your liking."

"Xerxes," said Alex, "you cannot treat this man like that. He is your host and has been very generous to you."

"Out of my way, boy," said Xerxes, and smacked Alex's face with the back of his hand. Alex fell to the ground, his cheek throbbing with pain and his lip cut wide open. Knowing it would mean his own death if he spoke again, Alex watched silently from a distance as Xerxes enacted the fullness of his wrath.

While Pythius looked on helplessly, his eldest son was dragged before Xerxes and forced to lie down on the ground. The young man's arms and legs were stretched out and tied securely to four posts. When this had been done, Xerxes ordered his executioner to make ready his ax. Most of those in the crowd expected that the executioner would chop off the head of Pythius' son, but instead, he cut his body into two equal halves. Xerxes took these two halves and, as though he were laying two boundary stones, placed them on either side of the royal road.

Then, in full view of Pythius and his family, Xerxes forced his troops to march between the two halves of the severed body. Alex closed his eyes as he passed and swore silently that he would do all in his power to help the Greeks defeat this tyrant.

◆ ◆ ◆

As the wails and screams of Pythius's family faded out behind them, the unstoppable army of Xerxes continued their westward march toward Sardis. Once there, they restocked their supplies and headed northward along the coast of Ionia. After several days march, Alex saw ahead of him on the horizon a low-lying hill on which rested what seemed to be the remains of an ancient citadel. He had never seen it before, and yet, at the same time, it seemed vaguely familiar. Xerxes too saw the hill and seemed moved by the sight of it. In fact, the moment he saw it, he ordered his army to halt and make camp. Then, mounting a horse and taking with him only his closest advisors and generals, he advanced toward the citadel. Intrigued by the mystery and by his own strange feelings of déjà vu, Alex followed along.

"Behold," said Xerxes, when they had reached the citadel, "in this very place, Greece dared to raise her sword against Asia. With an armada of ships, she raided these shores, and by the aid of trickery and deceit, she tore down these once mighty walls. But time has a way of avenging old wrongs. Today it shall be Asia that shall send her fleet to Greece. In me, the Greeks shall see a new King Priam, but one who possesses the strength and the fury of Achilles."

"Priam!" said Alex, "Of course, I should have known it at once. We are standing in the shadow of the ruins of Troy. King Xerxes, you are right to compare yourself to Achilles rather than to Hector, for it is Achilles' wrath, and not the heroic patriotism of Hector, that spurs you on to your goal. Again, I tell you to beware. It was Achilles' wrath, and not the arrow of Paris, that destroyed him in the end. His mother, Thetis, warned him that if he took the life of Hector, his own death would follow shortly after. But Achilles paid no heed to her words. Indeed, after they had defeated the city, the Greeks, as if made drunk by the wrath of Achilles, did terrible things to the Trojans and to their temples. The gods punished the Greeks for their arrogance and lack of pity. They all had bad homecomings."

"Again, you dare to preach to me, boy?" said Xerxes, "Still, there is some truth in what you say. I know well the old tales and have heard that their victory at Troy marked the beginning of the end for the empire of the Mycenaeans. Perhaps …"

"Make way! Make way! The king's messenger approaches!" Alex turned his head just in time to see a man on horseback charging toward him at full speed.

"Your majesty," said the messenger as he dismounted and fell at the feet of Xerxes, "I come to you with news from the Hellespont."

"Excellent!" said Xerxes, "Many months ago I sent my best engineers to lay the cables for my bridge across the Hellespont. With the cables in place, it should not be too difficult for my men to complete the bridge. Tell me, messenger, how goes the project?"

"I wish that I had good news to give to your majesty, but I will not deceive you. Three days ago, a storm of great force rose in the Hellespont and destroyed the cables laid down by your engineers. Nothing remains of their work."

Whatever progress Alex had made in dissuading Xerxes from his wrath was blown away completely by the news of the storm. Like a man possessed, Xerxes grabbed the messenger by his hair and dragged him to his feet. "Return at once to the Hellespont," he said, "and order my engineers to lash the waters of the Hellespont three-hundred times with whips made of cable. As they perform the lashing, they are to repeat exactly these words: 'You evil stream, it is Xerxes who beats you for your insolence. What harm have I done you that you should destroy my bridge? Know this, I shall cross you no matter how furiously you rage against me. And when I have done, I shall issue a decree that no one in my kingdom shall offer you a sacrifice.' When the engineers have spoken these words and delivered the full number of lashes, they are to be dragged themselves before the army and beheaded, one and all."

"What madness is this, O king!" said Alex, "If you look to your right, you will see the river Scamander. On that fatal day when he took the life of Hector, Achilles, in the madness of his rage, fought the Scamander with his sword."

"Silence!" screamed Xerxes, "One more word from you, boy, and I shall have you instantly executed. You threaten me with the fate of Achilles. So be it! Achilles was a man of action and of strength, and is remembered as the greatest warrior who ever bore the sword. As he won this honor, so shall I win the honor of being the greatest king who ever ruled."

After Xerxes' rebuke, Alex wisely held his tongue for the rest of the march to the Hellespont. Instead of heading straight north, Xerxes led his troops in a northwesterly direction toward the city of Abydos (AH bee dos). There the Hellespont was at its narrowest, and there Xerxes ordered that his bridge be built. Alex had always been fascinated by the beauty and strength of the Golden Gate Bridge in San Francisco, but that architectural wonder soon faded from his memory as he watched with amazement the construction of the Hellespont bridge.

Xerxes, who never did anything in a small way, ordered that 700 of his ships be linked together by strong ropes. At first, Alex thought that the troops would be made to march over the ships, but he was wrong. Xerxes, afraid that the cables for his new bridge would once again be destroyed by a storm, intended to use the boats to shield his bridge. Accordingly, he ordered that 350 boats be strung out to the right and left of the cables. As Xerxes had hoped, the boats slowed down the current, and allowed the engineers first to lay down the cables and then to stretch wooden boards across them.

When the bridge had been completed, Xerxes sat himself upon his golden chariot and ordered that the troops begin their march across the Hellespont. No sooner did the first soldier step onto the bridge than the sun vanished, and the sky grew dark.

"O gods," cried Xerxes aloud so that his men could hear him, "I see by this sign you have sent us that the lands of Greece shall soon fall into eclipse next to the glory of the Sun of Persia." Alex thought to himself with a smile that it was Persia, not Greece, for whom the sign was intended, but he thought it best not to share his interpretation with the king.

Rather than cross the bridge with the first detachment, Alex decided to remain behind so that he could get a better sense of the full number of soldiers in Xerxes' army. What he discovered made his heart sink. For three days and three nights, the army of Xerxes—in an unending line—marched slowly and solemnly from the shores of Asia to the shores of Europe. After the first day, Alex lost count of the number of troops. It was too large even to be imagined. It was as if all of Asia were on the move. It struck Alex that the land of Greece could never feed such an army, much less try to stop it. And as for water: such an army would drink the rivers of Greece dry. It was a terrible thought indeed, but it also gave Alex a slight ray of hope. If Greece could hold the Persians back long enough, they would eventually be forced to return to Asia for supplies. The very land that they sought to conquer would prove to be Persia's greatest enemy.

As Alex watched the troops pass by him and cross the bridge, he saw that one of Xerxes' counselors was writing in his book the names of each nation and people group to whom the different contingents belonged. And as he wrote down the names, he recited them aloud. Some of the nations Alex recognized; others sounded strange and exotic to his ears: Persians, Medes, Cissians, Hyrcanians, Assyrians, Bactrians, Scythians, Indians, Parthians, Caspians, Sarangians, Arabians, Ethiopians, Libyans, Cappadocians, Paphlagonians, Phrygians, Lydians, Thracians,

Pisidians, Cabalians, Moschians, Colchians. On and on they surged, like waves that break on a beach, pushing back the sand and forever altering the shoreline. They were like names in a dream, and the people who marched were like figures in a dream.

Last in order were the Babylonians, and as Alex heard their name fall from the lips of the counselor, he thought of an ancient story from the Bible. Babel had once been a great city, the first city, in fact, to rise up on the earth. But those who built it were proud and arrogant. In their dark hearts, they despised the lordship of God and sought to build themselves a tower that would reach from the earth to the heavens. By such means, they thought to pull down God from on high and make themselves a memorial that would outlive the ages. But God saw the wickedness in their hearts and visited a great plague upon them. Though before this time mankind had spoken a single language, God, in his anger, divided their once common tongue. When the builders found that they could no longer communicate with one another, they abandoned their mad ambition and were scattered to the four corners of the earth. Their tower, never completed, would come in time to be known by the name of Babel, for there God had babbled their languages.

As Alex thought upon the army of Xerxes, he saw at once that they were a divided people, who shared neither a common tongue nor a common culture. They were a babble, a tangled, motley assortment of humanity united only by their fear of Xerxes and of his power. Greece, it seemed, would have yet another advantage over Persia: her shared language and culture. If only she could hold together in unity against the hodge-podge troops of the Persian Empire, she just might have a chance.

If only she could hold together ...

Chapter 20

The New Bride

While Alex pondered the unity of Greece, his sister, Stacey, mourned quietly her separation from her brother. Indeed, they were now separated, not only by a thousand miles, but by the additional wall of twenty-four months. In keeping with his word, Hercules had transported Stacey two years into the future and then had left her at the base of that very fountain where Alex had awoken on the morning he had left for the Hellespont. Like her brother, Stacey had hoped that Alex would be beside her when she woke, and, like her brother too, she felt a stab of loneliness when she discovered that she was alone. Her brother's presence was something Stacey had always taken for granted; that a time would ever come when he would not be there to protect her and to explain things to her was a thought that had never once crossed her mind. Through all her trials, all her fears, all her joys and disappointments, Alex had always been there. He had been her anchor. But now that anchor had been removed, and Stacey felt adrift in a strange sea with no map to steer by and no star to guide her.

"Stacey," said a voice behind her, "Are you ready to meet Xerxes?"

"Who said that?" said Stacey.

"It is I, Hercules."

"But where are you?" said Stacey, "I don't see you."

"Look behind you at the fountain."

Stacey turned and stared at the statue of Hercules. To her great surprise, she discovered that although the arms, the chest, and the legs of the statue were made of cold white stone, the face seemed made of flesh. As she stared more closely, she saw that the lips of the statue were moving and that words were coming out from them:

"Yes, Stacey," said the voice, "it is really me, or at least a part of me. I have come to warn you that Xerxes will soon be entering the garden. Make sure you do nothing to provoke him. He has recently returned in defeat from Greece and is in no mood to be trifled with."

"Hooray," shouted Stacey, "then that means that Alex must have been successful and that Greece has been saved from the Persian army."

"Well, yes and no," said Hercules, "You and your brother, though you are separated from one another by two years time are actually carrying out your missions simultaneously. You are living and acting in two different streams of time. In your stream, Xerxes has already been defeated by Greece; it will be your task instead to save the Jews from his wrath. In your brother's stream, the war between Greece and Persia has yet to be decided.

"You see, daughter, that greater river which flows into the future from which you and your brother came is actually formed by the mingling of two different streams, each of which proceeds from a different gate. The first gate is Greece; the second is Israel. If your world is to know that freedom which she treasures so highly, then neither gate must be allowed to be closed or destroyed by the enemies of liberty. Together, you and your brother shall throw open those Gates of Freedom and usher in a wave that will grow larger and larger until it engulfs first Europe, then America, and then the world."

Stacey hoped Hercules would tell her more, but his voice stopped abruptly, and, in less time than it takes to blink, the face of the statue grew rigid and cold. No sooner had the face on the fountain changed itself to stone than Stacey heard the footsteps of Xerxes behind her.

"What is this?" said Xerxes, "Do you dare return to my palace now, after Greece has defeated me. Where was your Oracle when the Greeks were drowning my ships? Have you been sent to mock me in my misery?"

"Mighty king," said Stacey, "the Oracle has sent me here not to mock you but to console you. Her message to you is that you must forget Greece and focus instead on your own mighty empire. If you do this, she promises you a long and prosperous reign over all the lands of Asia. Better yet, she has sent me to assist you in finding a new queen to replace Vashti. You are destined, O Xerxes, to wed a woman whose beauty and virtue shall bring you greater joy and triumph than any military victory could hope to bring."

"Your words, O daughter of the Oracle, have unlocked the gates of my heart. What better remedy could there be for my sorrows than the arms of a loving queen? This very day I shall issue a decree throughout my empire that the loveliest girls in the land are to be brought here to Susa. From these, I shall choose a new queen, and you, child of Delphi, shall assist me."

"It would be an honor, your majesty," said Stacey, "but let me give you this one piece of advice. Let the woman you choose have about her an air of mystery. Let there be in her eye a distant look, as if she longed for something just out of reach. Let her seem like a princess who has lost her kingdom and her country, yet yearns for another that she cannot see."

"Yes," said Xerxes, "I see her even now in my mind's eye. Come, let us find her."

❖ ❖ ❖

As you can imagine, the servants who worked in the household of Xerxes got little sleep over the next few months. Every day, a new batch of dark-eyed beauties from the farthest reaches of the empire would arrive at the steps of the palace. Some were sweet and demure and cooperated nicely with the servants. Others were arrogant and deceitful and did all they could to sabotage their fellow "contestants." Stacey herself interviewed every prospective bride, hoping that she would come upon Esther. But this proved no simple task. Stacey knew better than to ask directly which girls were Jewish and which were not. She could tell by the snatches of gossip that she overheard that the Jews were not a favored people

The New Bride

in the empire and that many harbored feelings of envy and hatred toward them. She would have to very careful.

For Stacey, the best part of the search for Xerxes' bride was supervising the beauty treatments. Rich Persians were very particular about how their wives looked, felt, and smelled, and they would spare no expense in bathing them in the finest oils and perfumes. If Xerxes' first impression of a prospective bride was positive, he would order that she be taken to his harem and given a full month of beauty treatments. Stacey, to her great delight, was given the task of choosing just the right oils and perfumes for each girl. She also selected the exact colors that would be used to paint their lips and eyes. When all had been done properly, Stacey would complete the treatment by brushing and styling their hair with a set of ivory combs.

One day, while Stacey was soaking herself in one of the hot, perfumed baths, she heard the sound of a woman singing in a voice that could melt the stoniest heart with its sweetness. These were the words she sang:

> O heart within me, why are you so troubled?
> Why, O my soul, do you find no peace?
> My voice cries out in the day, but no one hears my calling,
> My whispers echo in the night, but they are not heard.
> Come quickly and rescue me, O lover of my soul,
> Do not delay, anointed one.
>
> I said that I would fly to you in my longing,
> I promised I would run and not grow faint;
> I said that I would ascend the hill that stands
> between you and me,
> And scale the heights that hide your face from mine,

But when I began my ascent, I was driven back to the earth;
When I struggled to rise, I was beaten down again.

Lead me, beloved, to the place of green pastures,
Guide my hand, until I come into the fold.
Do not forsake me in a house of strangers,
Do not leave me stranded in a foreign land.
For I am your bride who has sinned and returned,
And you are the bridegroom who ever forgives.

As she listened to the song, tears rose in Stacey's eyes, and she longed in her heart to return to her home and family. Gently, so as to make no noise, Stacey stepped out of the bath and put on a purple robe. Looking both ways to make sure no one else could hear her, Stacey bent down and put her lips near the ear of the woman who had been singing.

"Listen carefully," she said in a whisper, "I am a friend of the people of Israel. I can tell by the words of your song, and by the way you arrange them in pairs, that you are of Jewish blood. Your music and your poetry are like that of King David. If you feel you can trust me, then tell me your name."

"My Hebrew name," she said, "is Hadassah, but in Persia I am known as Esther. My uncle Mordecai (MORE de kai), who is more a father than an uncle to me, works here in the palace. It was he who summoned me to Susa to display my beauty before the king. But who are you that you should be a friend to me and my people?"

"My name is Stacey, and I have been sent here by the God you worship in secret to protect you and your people from a great danger that is to come. I can tell you no more at present, but please believe that I will help you in any way that I can."

The New Bride

"Then you come at an opportune time," said Esther, "for this very night I am to be taken to the royal bedchamber of Xerxes. Tell me, Stacey, what must I do to please him and to win his heart?"

"Esther," said Stacey, "you cannot imagine how I have longed to meet you. You are even lovelier than I thought you would be. But you will not win the heart of Xerxes by physical beauty alone. You must show him, as well, the beauty of your soul. When he calls you to his side and asks you what it is you most desire, you must answer that your greatest wish is to help him to forget the pain of the past and to look forward together to a future of joy. You must allow him to look deep into your eyes and to see there your hunger for peace and home. Xerxes is a rash and angry man; you must calm the heart within him with gentle words. Play your harp for him and sing of the yearnings you feel; let him share in those yearnings.

"Now go, fair Esther, and may the God of your fathers walk beside you."

✦ ✦ ✦

By nine o'clock the following morning everyone in the palace knew that Xerxes had found his bride. Stacey had never seen such joy in his eyes. He looked like a new man. Stacey was put in charge of the royal wedding and was even allowed to choose the food for the banquet. Xerxes proved a most wonderful host and lavished food and gifts on all the inhabitants of Susa.

To make the occasion even more auspicious, Esther's uncle, Mordecai, overheard two men speaking at that banquet who were friends and spies of the former queen, Vashti. Angered at Xerxes' decision to marry Esther, they planned to assassinate Xerxes on his wedding night. But Mordecai warned Esther of their evil plot, and she in turn warned Xerxes. Without disturbing the banquet, the two traitors were quietly arrested and executed.

With Stacey's help, Esther and her uncle had risen high in the eyes of Xerxes. At least one of the Gates of Freedom, it seemed, was secure.

Chapter
21

The True Path

While Stacey was enjoying herself at the wedding of Esther and Xerxes, Alex was slogging his way through the endless lands of Thrace and Macedonia. It is probably a good thing that he did not know what Stacey was doing. If he had known, he would most likely have wasted several hours a day stomping his foot, scowling, and proclaiming loudly: "it's not fair!" And of course, if he had, he would have been partly correct. There were no hot oil baths or rich banquets on the long road to Greece: just marching and marching and more marching. Still, Alex was able to lift his spirits somewhat by borrowing a horn from the military musicians and playing Sousa marches as he trudged along.

After proceeding for weeks in a straight westerly direction, the army finally turned south and headed down into Greece proper. Alex had hoped that Xerxes' army would meet some resistance as it pressed southward through Thessaly, but no such resistance ever appeared. One by one the city-states of Thessaly surrendered to Xerxes and turned over their men and supplies to Persia. If there were some within the city who hesitated, then a traitor or two would always rise up and open the gates during the night so that the Persian army could march in. The few Greeks who absolutely refused to surrender ran off into the hills and lived as rebels and bandits. With each passing day, it became more and more clear to Alex that if the Spartans could not hold back the army at Thermopylae, all of Greece would be overrun by the Persians.

The time had come for Alex to break away from Xerxes' camp and make his way to Leonidas and his Spartans. But this would be no easy task. Though Xerxes had become too engrossed in his battle plans to pay much attention to Alex, Demaratus, who was far less certain than Xerxes that the Persians would defeat the Greeks, kept a close eye on him at all times. He was by nature a suspicious man and could tell at once that Alex was up to something. Though Demaratus rarely spoke to him, Alex could always sense his presence and could almost feel the pressure of Demaratus's eyes watching him from the shadows.

One evening, while Alex sat warming himself by the fire, he sensed, as always, that Demaratus was not far away. Gathering up all his nerve, Alex cupped his hands around the sides of his mouth, and called out loudly into the night: "Demaratus, I know

The True Path

that you are close by. Come sit here with me by the fire. I have some questions I would like to ask you."

Demaratus, who was, to be honest, in a bit of a talking mood himself, moved out from behind a nearby tree and walked over to the fire. "Child of Delphi," he said, "if that is indeed who you are, I see that you are not one who is easily intimidated. The night is young, and I feel no desire for sleep. Ask your questions, and if they are the kind that I can answer, I will do my best to enlighten you."

"Well," said Alex, "I've heard many stories about the toughness of the Spartans, and I hoped you could tell me if they were true. For instance, I have been told that when Spartan boys are only seven, their mothers send them to live in the army barracks. There they are beaten by the older boys and are forced to steal their food and clothes."

"These things you have heard are true," said Demaratus, "My own mother did the same to me when I was seven. While in the barracks, we were given neither pillows nor blankets, but were forced to sleep outside with nothing to protect us from the cold and the rain. And it is true that we were expected to steal our own food, but woe to those of us who got caught! I remember once that a boy my age had stolen a fox for his dinner, but before he could kill it, he spied a troop of older Spartans coming our way. Quickly, so as not to be caught stealing, he took the live fox and hid it underneath his cloak. The soldiers spoke with us for an hour, during which time the boy gave no indication that there was a fox pressed against his belly. But when the soldiers left us, and the boy lifted up his shirt, I saw to my horror that the fox had eaten a hole right through his stomach. It must have been unbearably painful, but not once did the boy cry out or make a face. He was more afraid of the soldiers than he was of the fox's teeth and claws."

"But that's horrible," said Alex, "how could they treat their children that way?"

"It is our tradition," said Demaratus with a note of resignation in his voice, "it is the way things have always been done. I remember when I first left Sparta to fight in a war with our neighbors that my own mother handed me my shield. As she did, she spoke five words: with this or on it. What she meant was that I must either come back victorious holding the shield in my hand or be carried back dead inside of it. You must understand, boy, Spartans do not retreat. Even in the face of death, it is forbidden that we should throw down our shield and run for safety. We fight as a unit, shoulder to shoulder, and no one, on pain of death, would dare to break the line."

"But if the Spartans are so strong, then why don't you abandon Xerxes and fight alongside your people? From what you say of them, the Spartans have the will and the strength to stop Xerxes' army."

"You speak, my son, out of ignorance and the innocence of youth. I was exiled from Sparta by my own people; I can never return. Xerxes has treated me well, even if he laughs at me when I warn him of the fighting power of the Spartans, and has promised to restore me to my throne. I have chosen my course of action and cannot go back."

"That's not true," said Alex, "it is never too late to change and to choose again the right path. Xerxes is a tyrant, and you know it. It is not just Athens that he wants to punish. He won't stop until he has conquered all Greece and enslaved her people. How can you help him to do this?"

"I can only go where my fate leads me," said Demaratus, "and for now, it leads me in the path of Xerxes. Besides, though the Spartans have courage and skill, they care little for the rest of Greece. No Spartan will give his life to save Thebes or Athens or Corinth. They care only for Sparta and the lands around it. It is best that this war end quickly. Once Persia has united Greece under her Empire, Greece will prosper from the stability and the trade."

"But what about Greece's destiny? She too has a fate and a purpose. It will be Greece that will teach the world that men can live free without tyrants to control them. Athens knows this, even if Sparta does not. And I believe that you know it too, Demaratus. Before tonight, I had thought you were just a Spartan version of Hippias—a tyrant plain and simple who cared only for power and wealth. But I see now that you are different. You are not evil; you have just lost your way. Growing up in the barracks of Sparta has taught you to see only the bad in man; it made you bitter and caused you to despair. You thought that all men were liars and that no one could be trusted. But despite it all, there still burns within you a faith and a hope that mankind is nobler than that. Though you work in the camp of Greece's greatest enemy, you have not completely lost your honor and your nobility.

"Demaratus, it is my sworn purpose to leave camp tonight and travel to Thermopylae. There I shall meet with Leonidas and do my best to convince him to hold the pass. I know that you cannot accompany me in this task, or even help me, but it is my firm belief that you will not try to stop me. Though you have tried to convince yourself otherwise, you know as well as I that Greece can and *must* win this war. When I called you over to the fire, Demaratus, it was my plan to distract you for a second and then hit you on the head with a tent spike. Now instead, I give you that tent spike. If I am to accomplish my mission, it will not be by deceit, but by reminding every son of Greece of his great and glorious heritage.

"So farewell, Demaratus. If what I have said means nothing to you, then you may call the guards and have them put me in chains. But I do not think you will do that. You too would like to know if the Spartans will stand strong at Thermopylae and defend a pass so far away from their city. The only way anyone will find out is if you let me go. Farewell, and may the Oracle show you the way back to your true path."

Slowly, and with as much dignity as he could muster, Alex turned his back on Demaratus and began to walk away from the fire. To be honest, he was only half sure that Demaratus would let him go, but he knew that the risk was worth taking. If Demaratus could be persuaded to let him go, then Greece would not only have gained a fighting chance against Persia but would have gained something far more precious: the *right* to be free. Every step he took seemed to take an eternity, but he gritted his teeth and pressed on. Meanwhile, behind him, Demaratus stared into the fire.

When morning dawned, he was still staring into the fire.

Chapter 22

A Snake in the Grass

The months that followed the wedding of Xerxes and Esther were wonderful ones for the inhabitants of Susa. Xerxes was so pleased with the beauty and virtue of his new queen that he suspended all taxes for a year and distributed free grain to all the people. Spurred on by the kind heart of Esther, he even initiated public works to help better the lives of the poor in the city. It was, indeed, a wonderful time, and for awhile, it seemed as if it would go on forever.

But no good thing lasts forever in this fallen world of ours. Even in the Garden of Eden there dwelt a snake who envied and hated the happiness of our first parents. So too in Susa there lived a cold-blooded man whose only source of joy came from the knowledge that he had power over others. Xerxes' authority he could accept, but the thought that there was any other man above him was hateful to him. Though he had a family, he had no friends, for to him, people were objects that one used in the game of power.

Through manipulation, lies, and deceit, Haman (HAY min), for that was the name of the serpent of Susa, had wormed his way into the counsels of the king. He knew well how to flatter men like Xerxes and how to play on their weaknesses and their flaws. One by one, he used his wit and his lying tongue to separate Xerxes from his most able advisors and his truest friends. Whatever goodness Esther was able to instill in her husband, Haman poisoned and corrupted. He played upon Xerxes as though he were a pipe, until Xerxes could no longer tell which ideas were his own and which had been planted in his brain by Haman. Esther sensed what was happening but felt powerless to stop it.

With each passing week, Haman's influence at court grew stronger and stronger. It was as if Xerxes had been hypnotized, as if Xerxes himself had become the snake and Haman the snake charmer. Still, for all his victories, the joy that Haman sought eluded him. Although everyone at court, sensing the control he held over Xerxes, would bow in the presence of Haman, there was one who would not bow. That one was Mordecai, the uncle of Esther. He saw through the evil and cowardice of Haman and would not abase himself before one so vile. Mordecai was a servant of the one true God of Israel, and though he recognized the kingship of Xerxes, he refused to give praise to a man like Haman. For this reason, Haman nurtured a grudge against Mordecai, and because he hated him, he came to hate all his people as well.

Now, if truth be told, even before he met Mordecai, Haman had hated the Jews. He had noticed that though the Jews were subject people of Persia, they held their heads high and carried themselves as though they were freemen rather than slaves. Being in his heart both slavish and cowardly, Haman, like all men of his type, envied and despised those who possessed the moral courage and inner dignity that he lacked. Much to his frustration, he saw those very qualities of courage and dignity in all the Jews he knew—but most of all in Mordecai. Indeed, Mordecai's presence at court was a constant reminder to Haman of the qualities he lacked; merely to see him in the garden or the throne room or the market was enough to cause Haman misery and pain.

In the end, Haman swore that he would not rest until he had wiped from the face of the earth not only the hated Mordecai but all of his people as well. Better yet, he would use the destruction of the Jewish race as the final and greatest bond that would unite his own fortune with that of Xerxes. If he could incite the king to issue a decree to kill all the Jews in his empire, that decree would both rid Haman of his rival and make Xerxes an accomplice in his great crime. After ordering such a massacre, Xerxes would be driven forever into Haman's dark counsels.

Not one to procrastinate when his own advancement was at stake, Haman approached the king on the very next day and addressed him thus: "O mighty king, I beg you to pay heed to my words. There lives in your empire a group of people known as the Jews. They are a race of troublemakers who know neither loyalty nor obedience. They have been a plague on many nations from the Canaanites to the Assyrians to the Babylonians. Wherever they go, they spread rebellion and discontent. If you were to rid the world of this troublesome people, then future ages would sing your glory. You might even use their destruction to strengthen your hold over the other nations who dwell in your empire."

"You are a wise man, Haman, and judicious with your words and your counsel. But tell me, how are we to carry out such an ambitious plan?"

Haman opened his mouth to reply, but before he could speak, Stacey rushed into the throne room and stood between Haman and Xerxes. For the last few weeks, she had been in the habit of spying on Haman whenever he spoke to Xerxes. She had long noticed the hatred between Haman and Mordecai and feared that Haman would try to poison Xerxes' mind against Mordecai and his people. In fact, she had prepared herself for just such a situation.

"Lord Xerxes," she cried, "do not listen to this man. He would lead you astray with his slippery words. These Jews of which he speaks are neither troublemakers nor rebels but are a people chosen by God to bring light into the world. God promised the founder of their race, a man named Abraham, that he would bless those who blessed him and curse those who cursed him; this promise has been kept. If it please your majesty, I would like to tell you two stories of these people, stories that show what happened to a great and ancient nation who first blessed and then cursed them.

"The nation of which I speak, O king, is one whose strength in her day rivaled that of your own. She is Egypt, the land of the Pharaohs and of the pyramids, of the river Nile and the barren

A Snake in the Grass

desert. There was once in the land of Egypt a Pharaoh who could not sleep, for he was troubled by strange visions and dreams. In his dreams, he saw seven cows, healthy and fat, feeding along the Nile. As one does in dreams, he tried to move toward the cows, but he could not reach them. He was only an onlooker on the scene. For many minutes he stared at them, admiring their roundness and their color. But lo, as he looked, seven more cows appeared who were as sickly and skinny as the others were healthy and sleek. They were more like skeletons than living things, a pile of old bones strung together in the shape of a cow. And yet, despite their starved condition, they seemed to have great strength. In one swift motion, the seven skinny cows leapt upon the fat ones and devoured them whole. The Pharaoh thought that surely this feast would alter the shape of the skinny cows, but it did not. After finishing their meal, they looked even more hollow and scrawny than they had before. The next night, the Pharaoh had the same dream, but with stalks of wheat taking the place of the fourteen cows.

"Convinced that his dreams were a warning of great danger to come, the Pharaoh summoned all the wisest men of Egypt to interpret his dreams. But none could do what he asked. Finally, in desperation, the Pharaoh commanded that a certain young man named Joseph be brought to him. Now this Joseph, your majesty, was a Jew, one of the twelve sons of Jacob, whose name God had changed to Israel. Jacob was himself the grandson of Abraham whom God had first called to leave his home in the region of Babylon and set out for that land that would one day be known as well by the name of Israel. Joseph had been betrayed by his own jealous brothers and sold into slavery in Egypt. But God prospered Joseph and made him a blessing to the master for whom he worked. Later Joseph was betrayed again and thrown into a prison, but even there, God prospered him, and he rose to be the chief steward of the jail. While in prison, Joseph had correctly interpreted two visions that troubled the dreams of two of his fellow inmates. One of those inmates was eventually made royal cupbearer, and it was he who told the Pharaoh of Joseph's gift for interpreting dreams.

"When Joseph had been told all the details of Pharaoh's dreams, he replied, 'O great and mighty pharaoh, I alone could not hope to interpret your dream, but with the help of the Lord God, who speaks to me even now, I shall tell you the meaning of your vision. The seven fat cows represent seven years of plenty during which the land of Egypt will bear an abundance of food. The seven skinny cows represent seven years of famine and drought that will follow upon the years of plenty and devour them. God has sent these dreams to warn you of the coming famine that you might prepare for it during the years of abundance. This then, pharaoh, is what you must do: during the seven good years, you must set aside your extra grain in great storehouses. Then, when the seven lean years come, you will not only have grain aplenty for yourself, but will be able to sell the excess to the peoples who lie around you.'

"Pharaoh was so impressed by Joseph that he made him his second in command, and put him in charge of building the great storehouses for the extra grain. During the years of famine, Egypt used that grain not only to draw to herself all the wealth of the surrounding nations but to convince those nations to sell even themselves to the Pharaoh in return for grain. By this method, Egypt grew great in power and might and ruled over all her neighbors. Pharaoh bestowed on Joseph both wealth and praise and gave to him and his people the rich and fertile land of Goshen as their own.

"For many years, the Jews lived in Egypt, where they prospered greatly and were a blessing to all those around them. But a day came when a new pharaoh, who knew nothing of Joseph, rose to power in Egypt. He, like Haman, envied the Jews for their skills and for their prosperity and made them into slaves. Over them he put harsh taskmasters who beat and humiliated them. Yet still they continued to grow in number. Finally, when the pain and outcry of his people had grown great, God raised up a deliverer to rescue them from the cruel Egyptians. His name was Moses and, though he grew up in the house of Pharaoh, he chose to stand beside his people in their misery. Through Moses, God ordered the Pharaoh to release the Israelites and let them go free, but he refused. To persuade Pharaoh to relent from his pride and folly, God sent through Moses a number of plagues on Egypt, but with each plague, Pharaoh only hardened his heart the more. Finally, God sent the worst plague of all: the angel of death. Into Egypt this dark angel swept with his sword held high; in a single night, he slaughtered the first born son of every Egyptian in the land. Great was the outcry that rose up the following morning, and Pharaoh, who had lost his son as well, ordered Moses and his people to leave Egypt. But when the Jews were several days away from the city, Pharaoh changed his mind and sent an army of soldiers on chariots to capture the Jews and put them all to death.

"As the Jews were traveling by foot, the Egyptians caught up with them swiftly and pinned them down with their backs against the sea. It was then, Xerxes, that God worked through Moses his greatest miracle: he parted the waters of the Red Sea so that his people might walk through the midst of the sea as if on dry ground. When the Egyptians saw the Jews safe on the other side of the river, they charged across on their chariots. Just then, Moses lifted his rod, and the seas closed upon the Egyptians, causing the wheels of their chariots to catch in the mud and their drivers, one and all, to drown.

"Lord Xerxes, I beg you to follow the model of the first pharaoh and not of the second. God fights on the side of the Jews, and he will punish any ruler or nation who dares to harm them. Even those nations whom God has used to punish his people have, in the end, paid for their harsh treatment of the Jews. If the stories of these two pharaohs do not convince you, then think well on the fate of the kings of Babylon. When Nebuchadnezzar heeded the advice of Daniel, a Jewish exile who served at his court, he and his nation prospered and grew. But when the last king of Babylon refused the advice of that same Daniel, he and his kingdom fell to the army of your grandfather, Cyrus the Great. Leave these people alone, O king: to fight against them is to fight against their God. Do not let the jealousy of Haman cause you to bring ruin upon your empire and yourself."

"Stacey," said Xerxes, "you have spoken well. How do you respond, Haman?"

"She tells pretty stories, indeed," said Haman, "but how are we to know that her words are true? No power on earth can split a sea in half; such things simply do not happen. Your majesty is too wise and learned to believe such fables. As for visions, your majesty does not need Jews to tell him the meaning of his dreams. You have your court Magi to perform such tasks. And what are dreams anyway? Nothing more than pictures that dance in our heads as we sleep. I speak to you of real life, Lord Xerxes, not of stories written to amuse children.

"Besides, what she has not told you is that these Jews are people who hold their own customs and traditions above those of every other nation. Does not your majesty wish to construct one great empire and nation to unite the entire world? As long as the Jews live, you will find this a difficult thing to do. They despise the ways of the Medes and the Persians, and of all other peoples. They pay no honor to the many gods of Persia, but care only for their one God whom they claim is the only God who truly exists. In their eyes, Xerxes, you are just a man like any other man.

"If this does not convince you, your majesty, then think of this. The Jews are a wealthy people who horde their gold in their homes. Eliminate them and their riches will fall to you. Indeed, if you will agree to issue the edict for the destruction of these people, I will myself pledge to put ten-thousand talents into the royal treasury."

Though Xerxes had been strongly affected by Stacey's stories, Haman's words caused the natural anger within him to rise to the surface. Haman, of course, had neither disproved Stacey's stories nor proven his own accusations, but the wily Haman knew this was unnecessary. Being a keen student of Xerxes' weaknesses, he merely planted in the king's mind the notion that there were people in his empire who despised his rule and his customs. Once that bitter seed was sown, Haman well knew, Xerxes' own in-bred suspicion and inner rage would do the rest.

As Stacey looked on helplessly, Xerxes' cheeks flushed red with anger, and his hands clenched themselves into fists. No longer could he be reasoned with. Whatever Stacey said now would only fuel his anger more.

"Guard," shouted Xerxes, "order my scribes to come to my chambers at once. I have a decree that must be written tonight.

Stacey and Haman, you may retire to your beds. Tomorrow the decree to eliminate the Jews will be copied and distributed to every region of my empire."

"To hear is to obey, my Lord," said Haman, and bowed low to the ground. Stacey, on the other hand, pressed her lips together, swiveled around on her feet, and marched out of the room in a huff. She had worked on her speech for three full days, and Haman had exploded it in a matter of seconds. There was only one hope left now: she would have to persuade Esther to speak to Xerxes and convince him to cancel his decree.

But would Esther agree? She had not yet told Xerxes of her Jewish heritage. If she remained silent, there was a good chance she would escape being killed with her people, but if she spoke up, she risked being killed as well. Hercules had told Stacey that within true beauty there lay a seed of courage. If the Jews were to be saved, she would have to find that seed.

Chapter
23

The Three-hundred Spartans

On the second morning after he had left the Persian camp, Alex reached the pass of Thermopylae. Ahead of him lay the specific task for which he had been called to ancient Greece, the task for which he had been preparing himself ever since Hercules had transported him back to the trial of Orestes. Soon he would be standing face to face with his great, great, great, great-grandfather. What would he say to him? How could he convince him to give his life for freedom: a thing that you could neither see nor taste nor smell? And how would he (Alex) measure up to his noble ancestor?

"Halt!" said a voice above him, "What business do you have here?"

The words had been spoken by a guard who stood on an outcropping of rock that overlooked the pass. He was heavily armored with a huge shield that covered most of his body and a long spear that he held poised by his right ear. On his face, there was neither smile nor frown, just a calm, unflinching look of resolution. One would have an easier time passing by a wild bear than by this man. There was about him a spirit and a presence that seemed as firm and immovable as the rock face itself.

Alex tilted back his head and called out to the guard in his loudest voice: "I have come to see Leonidas. I have been sent by Hercules, the greatest hero of Greece and the ancestor of Leonidas. I have news of the Persians that can only be spoken in the ear of your commander."

"You are welcome here," said the guard as he lowered his spear and began to descend the mountain toward Alex. For one so heavily armored, his movements were surprisingly light and graceful; he was almost more stag than man. Alex had never before seen such a mixture of strength and beauty. It made him think for a moment of Hector, Achilles, and the other heroes of the Trojan War. It made him think too of what Hercules had told him: that there lay within true courage a seed of beauty.

The guard led Alex up the mountain and into the heart of the Spartan camp. There he found men whom one might have mistaken for Olympic athletes. They were spread out over the top of the pass in groups of twos and threes, their swords and shields lying beside them on the ground. Some sprinted in place; others

The Three-hundred Spartans

practiced leaps and somersaults; yet others stretched their limbs. In the midst of this feverish activity, one of the soldiers, who seemed taller and nobler than the rest, separated himself from the main body and ascended a high platform made of rock. In a voice that carried with it its own authority, he called out to the men below him:

"Form ranks!"

Before Alex could take his next breath, the soldiers on the field took up their swords and shields and formed themselves into the shape of a giant rectangle. As though they were building a three-dimensional jigsaw puzzle, they placed their shields side by side until the men themselves disappeared behind the four-sided wall of shields. The man on the rock called again, and the shields parted slightly, just enough to allow each soldier to thrust his sword through the crack. From Alex's point-of-view, they looked like a great spiked tortoise.

Once his men had grouped themselves into their formation, the commander on the rock began to bark out a succession of signals. In response, the entire formation would move, now to the left, now to the right, now straight ahead. They moved as one man, never allowing their shields to slip or their spears to sink low. "It's like watching a human tank," Alex thought to himself, "I would hate to see one of those charging at me."

After drilling the men for a full hour, the commander ordered them to stand down. At once, they dropped their shields and spears and resumed their various exercises. Meanwhile, the guard stepped away from Alex and spoke in the ear of one of the soldiers. When the guard had finished, the soldier ran quickly up to where the commander stood on the rock. He too spoke something into his ear, and then pointed in the direction of Alex. The commander looked carefully at Alex, spoke briefly to the soldier, and then walked down the far side of the rocky outcropping on which he had been standing. The soldier rushed back to the guard and spoke to him in words loud enough for Alex to hear:

"Tell the boy that Leonidas will meet with him in his tent. I am to lead him there."

"I am ready to go with you now," said Alex, "The news I bring is urgent."

"Very well," said the soldier, and led Alex up and over the hill on which Leonidas had been standing. At the bottom of the hill, Alex saw a large tent flying a banner with the insignia of a lion upon it. The soldier parted the tent curtain, and then stepped aside to allow Alex to walk in. "Leonidas has requested to speak with you alone," he said.

Though Alex would much rather have walked in together with the guard, he took a deep breath, lifted high his chest, and strode forcefully into the tent. To his surprise, Alex discovered that the tent contained neither a bed nor pillows nor any other type of luxury. Leonidas, he would learn that night, slept on the rocks beside his men. The tent was not Leonidas's personal dwelling but a meeting place for counsels of war. In the place where a bed might have been, there stood a large sturdy table covered with maps and charts of every kind. Around the table were several wooden chairs, upon one of which sat Leonidas.

"Come forward, young man," said Leonidas, "and let me look at you closely. Yes, yes, I had hoped that it would be you. All last night I prayed that Hercules would send you to me, and now you are here."

"Leonidas," said Alex, "you speak as though you and I had met before."

The Three-hundred Spartans

"We have, my son, we have! Don't you remember? It was ten years ago, just a few days before the Athenians met the Persians on the battlefield of Marathon. You, your sister, and an adult runner named Pheidippides had come to Sparta to ask us to join Athens in the battle, but the elders refused your request because they were in the midst of a religious festival."

"Wait a minute!" said Alex, his eyes opening wide, "You were the young man who took my side in the debate. It was you who told the elders that the gods would understand if you broke the festival to send help to Athens. It was you too who told them that Sparta must use her strength to protect Greece from her enemies."

"Yes, that was me, though I must admit I was a bit too brash for my own good in those days. For ten years now I've tried to convince my people to open their eyes to the greater world around them and to see that their fortunes are tied to those of Greece. It was *your* words, young man, that first opened my own eyes to the need for Greek unity. You planted a seed in my heart that has continued to grow to this day. That is why I prayed to Hercules that he would send you to me again. But, first, please tell me what your name is and where you are from."

"The first question is an easy one to answer. My name is Alex. The second question's a bit more complicated. Let's just say that you have influenced me as much as I have influenced you. In fact, if it weren't for you, I would never have been born."

"I see, Alex, that you, like the Oracle, prefer to speak in riddles. Perhaps it is no coincidence that I have been struggling these past few days with a prophecy that some of our messengers carried back with them from Delphi. According to the Oracle, one of two things must happen soon: either the city of Sparta shall fall to the Persians or a Spartan king of the house of Hercules shall surrender his life."

"Leonidas," said Alex softly, "I have spoken with the Oracle and with Hercules, and I can assure you that you are the king spoken of in the prophecy."

"My heart told me as much. I neither fear death nor the pain that accompanies it; yet, I wonder how the sacrifice of a single man can save an entire city."

"It is not merely that you shall die, Leonidas," said Alex, "but that you shall prove to both Persia and Greece that you were willing to die for something bigger than yourself."

"And what is that thing, Alex?" said Leonidas.

"Freedom. Not just your freedom, nor even that of Sparta, but the freedom of all Greece. More than that, by dying for an idea that was most fully developed not in your own city-state but in that of Athens, you will show the world that freedom is a thing that transcends cities and cultures and nations. The act of courage you display on the battlefield will seal with blood the high value of that freedom; just so, the beauty of that act will live in the minds of generations to come, spurring them on to greater deeds."

"Your words move me, Alex, but tell me," said Leonidas, suddenly shifting the topic, "what do you think of my three-hundred Spartans? They are all members of my royal bodyguard, and each of them is worth at least half a dozen men. For this mission I brought with me only those who have living sons back in Sparta. My own son, whom I must say resembles you closely, also remained behind in Sparta with my wife, Gorgo."

"They are the noblest fighters I have ever seen," said Alex, "and each of them to a man will willingly follow you to the grave. You yourself must have known in your heart that you and your men would not return, or you would not have brought with you only those with living sons. You knew that this would be a battle from which none of you would return, and you wanted to ensure that your soldiers had living sons to carry on their names."

"What then shall I do, Alex?" said Leonidas.

"I knew a man once who was very much like you. He too found himself in a battle that he could not win, but he thought that the cause was just, and he knew that by giving his life for it, he could swing the tide of war in the direction of victory and freedom. That man, Leonidas, lived by a simple motto: Be sure you are right; then go ahead. That is my advice to you."

"You have won me over, Alex, but before I agree to hold this pass, you must promise me something. In Athens, there is a man who speaks as you do about the need for all Greece to unite against Persia. He, in fact, was one of the men whose vision and whose words convinced me to come to Thermopylae. He has built for Athens a great fleet of warships with which he hopes to defeat the Persian navy. He appointed me to slow down the Persian advance and thus give him more time to ready his navy for war and to convince his fellow Athenians to abandon their city and put all their efforts into challenging the Persians at a port called Salamis. In this narrow bay, he hopes he can outmaneuver the Persian ships and score a victory for Greece."

"I know the man of whom you speak," said Alex, "I have met him once before in the Temple of Apollo at Delphi. His name is Themistocles, and it is my belief, and the Oracle's as well, that he will prove the savior of Greece. But what is it exactly that you want me to do?"

"In addition to my three-hundred warriors, I have command of several thousand troops from other loyal cities in Greece.

With their help, we should be able to hold back the Persians for several days. Still, I fear in the end that the Persians will find some way to break through our lines. When that time comes, I will dismiss the other soldiers and stand alone with my three hundred. As long as we continue to hold the pass, you may remain here at Thermopylae, but when you see me fall and my men with me, you must not stay behind, but must flee to Athens. Once there, you must tell Themistocles what you have seen and help him to convince the Athenians to abandon their city for Salamis. Unless you can do this, Alex, my sacrifice and that of my men will be in vain. Themistocles must finish what we began. Swear to me that you will do this thing the moment you see my body fall to the earth."

"I swear it," said Alex, "by the blood of Hercules himself. All shall be done as you ask. Whatever it takes, I will find someway to get to Themistocles."

Chapter
24

For Such a Time as This

Stacey waited until all of Esther's servants and maids had left for the night before she entered into the queen's bedchamber. She wasn't quite sure what she would say, but she trusted that the words she needed would come to her in the proper time.

"Esther," she whispered, "are you still awake? I need to talk with you."

"Of course, Stacey," she said, "I always enjoy speaking with you and would gladly miss many hours of sleep in order to spend it in your company. But tell me, what brings you here at so late an hour? Is all well in the palace?"

"Alas, dear queen," said Stacey, "all is not well. Your people, the Jews, are in grave danger. Spurred on by that snake, Haman, Xerxes has decreed that all the people of Israel who live in his lands are to be put to death on the same terrible day. Even now he is dictating to one of his scribes the decree that will doom the Jewish race to extinction. Earlier this evening I tried to counter Haman's arguments and to speak out on behalf of the Jews, but Haman has poisoned Xerxes' mind and robbed him of all sense and balance."

"But why do you come to me with this news?"

"Because, my sweet Esther, you are the only person in all the empire who has the power and influence to save the Jews from the coming destruction. If you can speak to Xerxes and change his mind, your people might yet be saved, but if you remain silent, there is nothing that can be done to block this decree. You must act, no matter the danger to yourself."

"But, Stacey," said Esther, "you yourself know that it has been a month since the king has called me to his bedchamber. If I were to go to him now, without him having summoned me, it would mean my death. Remember what happened to poor Vashti when she refused to come when Xerxes called her. I have no power over the king."

"But you *do*, Esther," said Stacey, "You have more power than you think. Your beauty holds more charm, more life, more truth than all the persuasive words of Haman. Your beauty is as strong as the arm of Samson and as sweet as the psalms of David. It was given to you by God as a gift, not to be used selfishly but to bring joy and hope to others. God made the world perfect, but evil men like Haman have filled it with ugliness and hate. You must hold up before the eyes of Xerxes a different vision, one of kindness and mercy."

"But I'm afraid. What if he will not listen to me? What if he throws me in prison before I can even speak to him?"

"That, Esther," said Stacey, "is a risk that you must take. Have you never stopped to wonder why it is that you are here in this place at this time? Have you not asked why, out of all the women in his empire, Xerxes chose you to be his queen? It is no accident that you have been brought into the palace just when your people most desperately need an ally at court. God's timing is always right, Esther."

"But why would the Lord choose me for such a task?"

"Why did he choose Abraham or Isaac or Jacob? Why did he choose the nation of Israel to be his bride? God does not see things as man sees them, my queen. My father taught me that a long time ago by telling me a story from the Bible. It's always been one of my favorites. May I tell it to you?"

"Please do," said Esther.

"Well, as I'm sure you'll remember, the first king that God chose to rule over Israel was a man named Saul. Saul was a powerful warrior who stood a head taller than all the other men of his day. But he disobeyed God, and God chose in the end to tear the kingdom away from him and give it to another. To prepare for that day, God called to his prophet Samuel. 'Samuel,' he said, 'take with you a flask of oil and go to the house of Jesse. There you will find the man who is to be my new king, my new anointed.' Samuel wondered in his heart how he would know which of Jesse's sons was to be the new king, but he chose to trust God and to follow his orders. When he arrived at the house, he called out to Jesse in a merry voice: 'Come quickly, my friend! I have great news for you and your household. The Lord God has told me that one of your sons is to be his new anointed.'

"In response, Jesse called his seven eldest sons to come into the house. The first was a huge man with arms of steel and legs of iron. Both Jesse and Samuel thought that God would surely choose him to rule Israel, but as Samuel prepared to pour the oil of kingship on his head, the voice of the Lord spoke in his heart and told him that this one was not his anointed. One by one, Jesse had his six other sons present themselves before Samuel, but of each one Samuel only said: 'He is not the Lord's anointed.'

"When all seven sons had been presented to Samuel and the anointed still not found, Samuel turned to Jesse and asked, 'Do you have any other sons dwelling in your home?' 'Well,' said Jesse, 'I have an eighth, younger son, but he is a small man with a ruddy complexion. His name is David. I did not call him for he is out tending our flocks.' 'Please, Jesse,' said Samuel, 'you must send for him immediately.' Several minutes later the door opened, and David, his clothes and his hair covered with mud and bits of fleece, entered the room. No sooner did his shadow fall on Samuel than the prophet fell at the feet of David and declared: 'This one is the Lord's anointed.' 'But how can this be?' said Jesse, 'He is the youngest and smallest of all. Why would God choose him above his brothers?' 'Do not be deceived, Jesse,' said Samuel, 'God does not see as man sees. Man sees the outside, but God sees the heart.'

"Even so, you Esther, though you seem to be the smallest and weakest of all, have a heart that is pleasing to God. With that same heart, you have delighted your husband the king. Do not underestimate your power. Xerxes' love for you is real; it is perhaps the only real thing in his cruel, chaotic life. Your people need you now, Esther, even as they needed King David so long ago. It was for such a time as this that you were promoted to queen. You must act now and so fulfill your destiny. Your beauty is the key to saving your people, but if you cannot gather the courage to appear before Xerxes, then all your beauty will have gone to waste.

"If all that I have said does not convince you, my queen, then think on this. Again and again, God has saved his people from disaster. Whether or not you rise up now and do your part, God *will* find a way to bring deliverance. If that happens, the Jews will be saved, but you and your household will lose the glory that might have been yours."

"I will do as you say," said Esther, "I will go to the king and speak on behalf of my people. And if it means I must die, then die I shall. But will you help me, Stacey?"

"I will do whatever I can, dear Esther. But first, I have a plan of my own that will help to lift up the reputation of Mordecai. If we can restore Mordecai to the good favors of Xerxes, it will be a great blow against Haman and may make him act rashly."

"But how will you do this, Stacey?"

"Don't you worry about that, Esther. Your job now is to get as much sleep as you can so you will look well rested and beautiful tomorrow. I will come wake you in the morning and tell you if I have been successful in my plans."

❖ ❖ ❖

Though Esther, Haman, and Xerxes had forgotten it, Stacey remembered that on the night of the royal wedding, Mordecai had helped to foil a plot against the king. Stacey's plan was to find some way to remind the king of Mordecai's service. Luckily, being a girl of almost perpetual curiosity, Stacey had, over the past several months, successfully searched through every room of the palace. During one of those searches, Stacey had come upon a small library where Xerxes' scribes kept the royal records. Since she had always loved books, even before she could read them, she had already spent many hours hidden away in the library looking through the scrolls. She loved the smell of them and their rough, grainy feel, and she would even draw pictures in the margins when she was sure that no one was looking.

As soon as she left Esther's bedchamber, Stacey headed directly for the library. Xerxes' father, Darius, had taught him to keep careful account of all that passed in his realm, and Xerxes had accordingly ordered his scribes to write down whatever happened of note in the palace. On the off chance that one of those scribes had recorded how Mordecai had foiled the plot to assassinate the king, Stacey did a quick search through the scrolls for that year. As she had hoped, she found a scroll that described Mordecai's service to the king in exact detail. Taking it firmly in hand, Stacey stole out of the library and made her way to the wine cellar.

Now, to the typical observer, Stacey's decision to go to the wine cellar might seem peculiar indeed. But then you must remember that Stacey had done a very thorough search of the palace and had unlocked all of its secrets. And one of those secrets just happened to involve a hidden passageway that linked Xerxes' bedchamber to the wine cellar. Up that passage Stacey now crawled with the royal scroll suspended between her teeth. When she found that she could no longer crawl forward, she reached out her hand and, with a slow, steady motion, slid back the panel that led into Xerxes' room.

Stacey heard at once a great grinding sound that almost caused her to dash back down the passage. As it turned out, it was a good thing that she did not follow this course of action. If she had, she would not have realized, as she did a moment later, to her great relief, that the grinding sound was a good omen: it meant that Xerxes was fast asleep and snoring peacefully! Taking off her shoes, she tiptoed her way over to a large table that stood at the foot of the bed. Carefully, she spread out the scroll on the table and then retraced her steps back to the panel.

Before leaving the wine cellar, Stacey had placed in her pocket a large, heavy cork that had been removed from one of the bottles. Stacey now took up that cork and hurled it with all her might at a round gong that stood to the side of the bedchamber and which Xerxes would strike twice if he wished to summon a servant to his room. Then, as quickly and as quietly as she could, she slid the panel closed and crawled back to the wine cellar. The gong, meanwhile, clanged loudly and caused Xerxes to sit up suddenly in his bed. Leaping to his feet, Xerxes began to pace the room in search of intruders. When he realized that there were no intruders to be found and that he could not even determine what had caused the gong to go off, he began to wonder if he had not dreamed the whole thing. Seeing no reason to pursue the matter, Xerxes returned to his bed with the full intention of resuming his interrupted sleep. As he prepared to do so, however, his eye caught sight of the scroll that Stacey had placed on the table. Not remembering having seen the scroll there the night before, Xerxes took it up in his hands and inspected it carefully.

He realized quickly that the scroll recounted the months surrounding his wedding to Esther. As this was a period in his life for which he had particularly fond memories, Xerxes decided that instead of going back to sleep, he would read through the scroll. And that was exactly what he did.

Chapter 25

Leonidas's Last Stand

Not one to hide anything from his men, Leonidas, once he had finished his talk with Alex, marched back up to the rocky platform from which he had earlier drilled his troops. In a voice filled with the rough joy of battle, he shared with them publicly his final and irrevocable decision to face the Persian army. Being the brave soldiers that they were, the three-hundred Spartans, one and all, cheered their leader's decision and pledged their lives to the coming struggle. The sight filled Alex with hope and made him feel that perhaps these mighty warriors could beat the Persian army all by themselves. Perhaps they would not need to sacrifice their lives. Perhaps they would survive to share in the celebration of a Greek victory over Persia.

For the remainder of the day, Alex watched in awe as the Spartans continued their preparations for battle. Their strength, their agility, their precision were almost beyond belief. Each on his own would have been enough to defeat a dozen men, but when they were combined into a single fighting unit, they become something even greater: something close to a force of nature. And at the eye of this human hurricane—calm, still, immovable—stood Leonidas. It was his force of will and command that held together the swirling energy of his men, that harnessed and organized it into a weapon for defeating the enemy. According to Greek mythology, it was Zeus alone who wielded the thunderbolt and who had the power to hurl it at whomever he chose. As Alex watched the Spartans practice on the field, he realized that Leonidas too possessed this power, that what he wielded was as swift and unstoppable as a thunderbolt.

As evening approached, the Spartans put down their weapons and turned their thoughts to dinner. I can't say that the food they ate was particularly tasty, but they ate it nonetheless. The belief that eating is one of the great pleasures of life, a belief shared by every modern Greek, was not, I am afraid, a belief held by the ancient Spartans. In fact, the thousand little pleasures and luxuries that the Athenians so loved were all but unheard of in Sparta. Perhaps that is why Alex was even more shocked than he might normally have been when he noticed that each of the soldiers, after he had finished eating, poised himself upon a rock and began to comb his hair. Indeed, more than merely comb the thick, dark locks that curled around his head, each groomed every inch of his body, spreading olive oil liberally on his arms and legs and smoothing out every hair. It was like watching a pet owner groom his poodle for a dog show, with the exception, of course, that it was his own body that he was grooming.

Alex's first reaction to this was the same reaction that most eleven-year-old boys would have had: disgust. "Are these men or little girls?" he thought to himself, "The next thing you know, they'll start putting on make up!" Finally, when he could take it no longer, Alex stormed over to Leonidas and asked him why his men were acting in this shameless manner. Alex was unprepared for the answer. "Do not think, Alex," said Leonidas, "that they are indulging in vanity or putting on airs. The reason they are anointing their skin with oil and combing their hair is that they are readying themselves for death. They know that it is unlikely that they will survive the battle tomorrow, and, as their wives are too far away to prepare their corpses for burial, they are doing it now themselves."

Feeling a bit foolish, Alex asked if he could go to bed. Leonidas gave his permission and even let Alex sleep in his tent. Alex thanked him and entered the tent, but in truth he got very little sleep. All night long, he kept seeing in his mind's eye the Spartan soldiers bravely and serenely preparing their bodies for the grave. He had never known that such courage existed, that there were people who could look so calmly into the face of death. In the end, he drifted off to sleep, but his dreams were troubled by visions of troops of soldiers marching unflinchingly into a wall of fire. And at the center of the troop was a gigantic man whose enormous head bore three different faces. The first face was that of Hercules; the second that of Leonidas. The third was dim and shadowy, without features or color, but Alex recognized the shape of the forehead and the curve of the chin. The face was his own.

The Gates of Freedom

✦ ✦ ✦

Everyone expected that the battle would begin the following morning, but it did not. Though Xerxes' army had reached Thermopylae and stood poised and ready to attack, it neither moved forward nor issued a threat. For four days this strange stalemate continued, until a spy managed to make his way to Leonidas and tell him what was happening. Xerxes, it seemed, was so certain that the Spartans would abandon their posts when they saw how large his army was that he decided to wait and let them leave rather than risk losing men in an attack. Xerxes never considered for a moment that anyone would be brave enough, or foolish enough, to hold the pass against such an overwhelming enemy. Of course, Leonidas and Alex were overjoyed by this four-day stalemate. Every day that the Persians delayed gave Themistocles another twenty-four hours to organize the rest of the Greek city-states.

But when, on the fifth day, Xerxes saw that the Spartans would not leave, he was seized by a wild fit of anger and ordered his generals to sound the attack. Still refusing to believe in the "myth" of Spartan invincibility, Xerxes began his assault on the pass by sending out, not his Persian forces, but lesser soldiers composed of Medes and other subject peoples. Indeed, in his rage and folly, he commanded the soldiers to capture the Spartans alive and to bring them to him unharmed.

This proved a rather difficult task.

Perhaps you have seen a movie in which a herd of buffalo stampedes over a grassy field. The Medes who attempted that day to capture the Spartans found themselves trampled as thoroughly and mercilessly as grass beneath the buffalo's feet. Again and again, Xerxes replaced the trampled Medes with fresh troops, but the Spartans mowed them down more quickly than they could be replaced. None of the Medes could break through the Spartan wall of shields. On the contrary, before they could get within three feet of the shields, they were stabbed to the heart by the Spartan spears that stuck out from between the shields. Those lucky enough to elude the spears would end up colliding with the shields with a force that sent them flying to the ground. Once on the ground, they would be treated to the horrific experience of being stepped on by the marching feet of a hundred Spartans. None survived the experience.

By mid-day, Xerxes had recalled the remaining Medes and sent on to the field his finest troops: the Persian Immortals. The Spartans would soon make them doubt their nickname.

Before the battle started, Alex had wondered why the Spartans carried such long spears when they attacked: spears so heavy and clumsy that Alex found he could not even lift one, much less run with it. As he watched the three hundred battle the Immortals, he quickly realized why. The Spartan spears were a full foot longer than those carried by the Persians, a difference that gave them a distinct advantage. In order to get close enough to stab the Spartans, the Immortals had to put themselves in harm's way. The Spartans, on the other hand, could kill the Persians without ever coming within range of their spears. This advantage, when added to the Spartan ability to fight in close formation and to swoop down on their enemy with incredible speed, allowed them to kill dozens of Persians with each charge.

The Immortals, whose training was as extensive as that of the three hundred, quickly realized that they would have to alter their strategy if they were to defeat their Greek foe. Accordingly, the next wave of Immortals, rather than rushing in a long thin line at the Spartans, slowed their attack and grouped themselves into smaller units. Each unit concentrated on a specific area of the Spartan wall of shields and attempted to find a gap which they could use to split open the formation. At first, the Persians proved unsuccessful. In addition to their heavy spears, the three hundred wore heavy armor that protected them in close combat. (Much of the rigorous training the Spartans endured was done with the sole purpose of empowering them to hold up under the weight of their armor and spears!) Still, they couldn't hold out forever. With each passing moment, the Immortals pushed in closer, and even managed to stab several Spartans with their daggers. Alex feared the battle would soon be over, but Leonidas wasn't so willing to concede a quick defeat.

In the midst of the struggle, Leonidas called out a single command. Immediately, every Spartan swiveled on his heels and began to run away from the Immortals at top speed. This sudden turn of events puzzled and even angered Alex a bit. Were the noble three hundred running away? The Immortals, thinking the same thing, lifted high their spears, let out a war cry, and began to chase after the Spartans. The chase did not last long. Just when the Immortals were reaching full speed, Leonidas called out again, and the Spartans stopped dead in their tracks. Once again, they swiveled on their heels until they were facing the oncoming enemy. The sight shocked and terrified the Persians who tried their best to stop and swivel with the same speed and agility as the Spartans. They were, of course, unable to do so. Before a single Persian could turn and run, the Spartans were upon them like a tidal wave. One minute there was a battalion of one-thousand Immortals standing on the pass; the next minute they were gone, trampled underfoot by the Spartan machine.

By the end of the day, the pass was strewn with the bodies of ten-thousand soldiers from every corner of the Persian Empire. Xerxes had opposed Leonidas with troops from a dozen different nations, but none could hold out against the Spartans and their allies. Spurred on by the three hundred, the other soldiers who had come to Thermopylae from various Greek city-states proved that they too knew the meaning of honor and valor and that they too could inspire fear in their enemy. Indeed, as Xerxes' hodge-podge army was pulled further and further apart along religious and ethnic lines, the Greeks only grew more united in spirit and mind.

"At this rate," thought Alex, "the Greeks really may defeat the Persians and send them running back to the Hellespont."

Alas, Alex had forgotten a lesson that he himself had taught the Oracle: namely, that the internal enemies of freedom are often more dangerous than those on the outside.

✦ ✦ ✦

For the Christian, there is no name more hated than that of Judas; for the American, it is Benedict Arnold who holds that distinction. In Europe during the Second World War, it was a man named Quisling. The ancient Greeks, too, had their traitors—Hippias standing quite high on the list—but of all those who betrayed their country to the tyrants of the East, none was more despised than Ephialtes (eff ee ALL teeze).

As Alex stood upon an outcropping of rock and watched with joy each successive Spartan victory, his heart filled with thoughts of courage and freedom. On another hill, not far away, a very different man watched the progress of the battle, but it bred in him sinister desires for Persian gold. To the twisted mind of Ephialtes, the struggle at the pass meant only one thing: a chance for profit and untold wealth. That night, while the armies of Sparta and Persia slept soundly, Ephialtes stole his way into Xerxes' camp with a proposition. For a dozen bags of silver and gold, he would lead the Immortals up a secret goat path along the steep sides of the pass. The path would allow them to sneak around the Spartans and to position themselves behind and above the pass of Thermopylae. Once there, they could attack the Spartans from the rear while the rest of the army charged at them from in front. The Greeks would be surrounded; they would have no choice but to surrender.

Xerxes, more concerned now with winning than with fighting in an honorable fashion, accepted Ephialtes' proposition and put him at the head of a detachment of three-thousand troops. By the time the Spartans woke to renew the battle, they had already lost it. Before noon on that fateful day, the word reached Leonidas that the Persians had found a way to circumvent the pass and were massing themselves on a ridge about a mile above where the Spartans were stationed. When Leonidas heard the news, his countenance sank and his complexion grew dark. But the change only lasted for a moment. As if a fire had been lit deep down in his belly, Leonidas's eyes suddenly sparkled, and his limbs began to pulse with energy:

"Spartans," he said, "the end draws near. The unthinkable has happened; a Greek traitor has betrayed us and shown the enemy the secret path that leads around Thermopylae. But that does not concern me overmuch. He will pay in the end for his treachery. For us, there is only one question: will we die with dignity or allow our honor to be smeared by the acts of a traitor. My fellow Greeks who have joined us from Thebes, from Corinth, from

Leonidas's Last Stand

Boeotia (bow EE sha), and from many other city-states, you have fought bravely and well, but the time has come for you to return to your homes. We Spartans alone shall remain and hold back Xerxes for as long as we can. It will be up to you to reach your cities safely and to spread the news of our last stand against the Persians. The future of Greece lies in your hands and in those of your countrymen whom you can spur to battle with your words."

Alex could see that many of the soldiers from the other city-states would have much preferred to remain and fight with the Spartans, but he could see as well that none of them would dare disobey the words of Leonidas. There could be no other way. It was their lot to live to fight another day as it was the destiny of the three hundred to make together the greatest sacrifice of all. What they did that day would be remembered down the ages, even by those who had never heard the names of Leonidas or Thermopylae.

Once the other Greeks had left the field, the Spartans did something they had not dared do before. Thus far, they had fought the Persians in the narrowest part of the pass. But now, with the knowledge that the Persians positioned above them would soon be swooping down at them from behind, the Spartans were averse to being confined in so narrow a space. If they were to die, they would die in the open field. When the Persian army saw that the Spartans had moved forward into the wider part of the pass, they rushed upon them with great speed. Without the narrow walls of the pass to protect their right and left flanks, the Spartans' formation was left vulnerable to being split open along the side. The Persians knew this and attacked them mercilessly. After an hour of close fighting, the Spartan wall of shields was split in four, then six, then eight. Still, they fought on.

Two hours later, the Spartans heard the sounds of shouting coming from behind them. Another ten minutes and they were surrounded on all sides by the armies of Persia. It was then that Xerxes rode forth and addressed the Spartans in words that mixed scorn with respect:

"Spartans," he said, "you have fought well and no one here can speak ill of your courage. But the struggle has been lost. I give you this one chance to surrender and thus save your lives. It is folly to persist. I have but to lift up my hand, and my archers will block out the sun with their arrows."

The Spartan response to Xerxes' taunt was immediate and final. Alex could never tell which of the three hundred had said it, but his words would remain with Alex for the rest of his life. "How pleasant," answered back the Spartan, "if the Persian arrows block out the sun, then we shall fight in the shade."

Enraged at the soldier's defiance, Xerxes lifted his hand and a volley of arrows fell upon the Spartans from every direction. Many Greeks died in that moment, but as many others deflected the arrows with their shields and continued the fight with renewed vigor. After another hour of close fighting, the Spartans found that all but a dozen of their long spears had been split and broken. But even this did not halt the fury of their assault. Dropping their now useless spears, they drew their daggers from their sides and engaged the Persians in single combat.

When even the daggers failed, they fought on with their hands and their teeth.

And then it came. A terrible cry that pierced through the air like the arrow of Apollo: "Leonidas is fallen." As Alex gazed down on the battlefield through his tears, he saw twenty Spartans rush to the side of their fallen commander and drag him from the midst of the fighting. Alex yearned to rush down to the field himself and to speak his final words to Leonidas, but in his grief, he remembered the promise he had made. Gazing around wildly for the best route of escape, Alex chose a path that led higher up the pass. For the first hundred yards, Alex moved swiftly and silently, and he began to hope that his escape would be an easy one. It was at that moment, of course, that he turned a corner to find himself face-to-face with half a dozen Persian soldiers.

At another time, Alex would have been so paralyzed with fear that he would have fallen to his knees and surrendered. But not today. Not only had he just witnessed first hand the bravery of Leonidas and the three hundred, but his promise to the Spartan commander burned with fury in his mind. Without thinking what he was doing, Alex bent down and picked up a walking cane that had been left lying on the ground beside him. Then, letting out a tremendous war cry, he charged headlong at the startled Persians. As he charged, he swung the cane furiously in the air. With a great cracking sound, the cane smashed against the cheek of one of the Persians and sent him flying to the ground. Another swirl of the cane, and Alex connected with the chest of one soldier and the belly of a second. The remaining three, now fully conscious of what was happening, spread out in different directions and then began slowly to close in around Alex.

Alex waited until they were almost within range of his cane, and then threw himself down. As he fell, he rolled over on his left shoulder and swung the cane sideways along the ground. The closest soldier, unprepared for Alex's move, caught the cane full on his left ankle. Alex, meanwhile, sprang back up to his feet and hurled the cane at the closest of the two remaining soldiers. The cane struck him in the nose and upper lip and sent him reeling backwards into the dirt. Hoping to retrieve his weapon, Alex lunged forward toward the fallen soldier, but before he could reach it, he felt a hand grab his shoulder from behind and pull him back up to his feet. Then, all in one swift motion, a thick, hairy arm wrapped itself around his two arms, pinning them to his sides, while a dark, oily hand pressed a dagger to his throat.

"I have never killed a boy before," said a rough voice in his ear, "but I shall enjoy slitting your throat."

Alex closed his eyes and awaited the cut, but instead, he felt the body of his would-be killer shiver and go limp. His arms no longer pinned, Alex spun around, and the dead body of the Persian fell forward into his arms. It took Alex only a second to figure out how the soldier had died. Sticking out from the middle of his back was the gilded hilt of a dagger.

Alex laid the body down gently and then searched the field for any sign of his rescuer. It did not take him long. Poised on a low-lying ridge about twenty yards away stood a man whose face and hair looked Greek but whose clothing was clearly Persian.

Alex recognized the man at once. It was Demaratus, the exiled king of Sparta.

Alex motioned toward Demaratus with a gesture of thanks that no words could express. In response, Demaratus spoke only these words:

"Go," he said, "and restore my honor by your own."

Still unable to speak, Alex saluted Demaratus once, then turned toward the mountains and ran.

Chapter 26

The Tables Turned

When Stacey woke Esther up on the following morning, she found, to her great delight, that sleep had not removed the edge from Esther's resolve. Even if it meant her death, Esther was determined to see Xerxes and plead for the life of her people. Not wanting to give Esther any false hopes, Stacey decided not to tell her about her nocturnal adventure in the bedchamber of Xerxes. Instead, she led Esther down to the royal baths and put her through an intensive, eight-hour beauty treatment. "Wow," thought Stacey, as she scrubbed and combed and painted, "this beauty business is hard work!" But when the treatment had been completed, and Esther came forth in the fullness of her beauty, Stacey forgot immediately the sweat and toil she had expended during the day.

There are some who think that the beauty of a woman is a thing that can be enjoyed only by the male of the species. Stacey learned that day the folly of such thinking. Just as all people, male or female, take delight in the strength and courage of the Olympic athlete or the fearless soldier, so all men and women who possess souls that have not yet been beaten down by ugliness and greed are subject to the charms of a lovely girl in her prime. When her eyes fell upon Esther, Stacey's mouth hung open with awe, and her heart beat quicker within her. Esther seemed to glow with the radiance of the moon and the stars. Everything that Stacey had ever learned about balance or harmony or proportion seemed to converge and to rest in the face and the figure of the queen. One could not look upon Esther without feeling both tenser and looser: the tension that comes when one anticipates a sought-after pleasure; the looseness that comes when a great weight or burden has been lifted.

As though she were walking in a dream, Esther glided through the rooms of the palace until she came before the door of Xerxes' private chamber.

"Guard," said Esther to the soldier on duty, "please inform Lord Xerxes that I desire an audience with him."

"Have you gone mad, my queen?" said the guard, "You of all people must know that it is death to appear before the king unbidden."

"Nevertheless," said Esther, "you must do as I ask. If the king's anger is aroused, then let his wrath fall on me alone."

The Tables Turned

"Very well, O queen," said the guard, "though I fear greatly for your life." Without another word, the guard opened the door and entered the chamber. Stacey and Esther held their breath as they waited to see how Xerxes would react. After what felt like an eternity, the door slowly opened, and Xerxes stepped out. His face appeared troubled, and for one terrible moment, he looked as he had looked on the night he had dismissed Vashti from his palace. But the bitterness and anger of that look melted away the moment his eyes fell upon Esther. What happened next can only be described as a kind of melting or softening that seemed to wash out all the lines of worry and wrath that had accumulated on his face over the last ten years.

"Esther," he said, "it is good to see you. I am glad that you have come. Not twelve hours have passed since I read again in the royal scrolls the account of our wedding. You appear to me now as you did on that night, but with a greater beauty and a richer charm. Tell me, my beloved, what is it that you would have of me? Whatever you ask I shall give it to you, even up to the half of my kingdom."

"My lord," said Esther in a voice as pure as the song of the nightingale, "if I have found favor in your sight, I ask that you come to my chamber tomorrow evening and dine with me. I ask as well that you bring with you the lord Haman, for I know that he is close in your counsels."

"With great joy, I shall do as you ask, and would fain do much more, for there is about you this evening a radiance that warms the blood within me."

"I shall wait for you, my lord," said Esther, "as the roses of morning await the dew."

❖ ❖ ❖

When Haman received Xerxes' invitation to dine with him in the chamber of Esther, he immediately ordered his servants to work all night on the construction of a gallows. Certain now that whatever he asked of Xerxes would be granted him, he planned to slander Mordecai before the queen and convince Xerxes to hang Mordecai from the gallows as a finale to their dinner. Not knowing that Esther was the niece of Mordecai or even that she was of Jewish blood, he thought, in his folly, that Esther would be pleased by the hanging. Why else would the queen have asked for him specifically? Surely she knew of his plans to destroy the Jewish people and was in agreement with them. Surely she would reward him for helping her husband to rid his empire of the threat of Mordecai and his people.

Such are the private thoughts of a scoundrel and fool.

❖ ❖ ❖

With Stacey in charge of the food and entertainment that evening, and Esther looking, if it were possible, even more lovely than she had the previous night, Xerxes soon fell into a state of joy and peace that he had not known for many months. "Esther," he said, as they finished their meal, "tonight you have pleased me with your beauty and your hospitality. No husband has ever been blessed with such a wife as yourself. Therefore, ask me now whatever you will, and it shall be granted you, even on to the half of my kingdom."

"My lord," said Esther, "for myself I ask nothing but to serve and please you for all of my days. But there is a thing that I would have you do, not only for me, but for you and your kingdom. An edict has been decreed that all the Jews in Persia are to be put to death on the same day. Do not carry out this decree, my lord, for it is my belief that these Jews whom you would kill are loyal subjects and keepers of the peace."

"The queen does not know what she is saying," said Haman, who was caught unprepared by the queen's request, "These Jews are neither loyal nor peaceful. Each and every one of them would plunge a dagger into your back if he were given the chance. No, Lord Xerxes, though I honor your wife above all women, I tell you that she has been misinformed about the nature of the Jews. I swear to you, O king, that there is not in all your kingdom a Jew who is loyal to you or your throne."

"There is!" said Esther, "I am a Jew!"

"How can this be," cried Xerxes, now staring at Esther, now at Haman, "is it possible, my queen, that you are one of these people whom I have sworn to kill?"

"I am."

"This is insanity, your majesty," said Haman, "Esther is no more Jewish than I am. It is clear to me that she has been bewitched into believing it by the most foul traitor in all Susa. I speak of an evil and deceitful man named Mordecai. This very day, my servants have completed the construction of a gallows from which to hang Mordecai. I implore your majesty that the execution be carried out …"

"Silence," roared Xerxes, his face flushed with anger, "first you set my sword against my wife's people, and now you dare to slander one who is a favorite of the king. On the very eve of my wedding to Esther, this Mordecai, whom you call a traitor, uncovered an assassination plot against my life. Only yesterday I read the account in the royal scrolls. In all my lands, there is no man more loyal than Mordecai. Indeed, he shall be lifted up, but not on your gallows. From this very moment, all your lands and wealth, Haman, are to be given to Mordecai and his descendants. As for you and your family …"

But Xerxes could not finish his sentence. So confused and enraged was he by Haman's words that he walked swiftly out of Esther's chambers and into the enclosed garden. The moment he was gone, Haman rushed over to where Esther was seated, bowed low before her, and begged her to intercede with him before the king. Esther turned her face from the traitor and looked instead at Stacey.

Stacey, meanwhile, hit upon a plan to rid the Jews forever of their greatest enemy. "Forgive me, dear Esther," she whispered, "but I've had all I can stand of this two-faced whiner." With that, Stacey rushed over to where Haman was standing and landed a swift kick on his well-padded backside. The kick sent Haman flying forward, and he fell face down on top of the queen. The impact of Haman's body caused the queen to let out a single cry.

Immediately, Xerxes rushed back into the room and saw Haman spread out on top of his wife. "Will this vile man even molest my queen?" he cried, "Guards, bind Haman fast and see to it that this very night he is hung from the gallows his servants built for Mordecai. I had thought to show him mercy and spare his miserable life, but he is not fit to live another hour."

With wails and shouts more shrill than any alley cat could produce, Haman was dragged from the queen's chamber. Xerxes invited Esther and Stacey to witness the hanging of Haman, but both ladies declined. Each closed the shutters of her bedchamber tightly so that they would neither hear nor see the wretched end of the wretched Haman.

The Tables Turned

The next day was one of great feasting and celebration throughout the empire. Xerxes rescinded his decree to kill the Jews and lifted up Mordecai to the highest position in his court. In all Susa, only Xerxes commanded more honor and respect than Mordecai.

As for Esther—well, as Stacey always liked to say, she lived happily ever after.

Chapter 27

The Wooden Walls

It wasn't until he had reached the highest peak in the mountain range through which cut the pass of Thermopylae that Alex realized he could never fulfill his promise to Leonidas. He had told the Spartan commander that he would personally carry the news of the Spartan defeat to Themistocles in Athens, but Athens, it suddenly dawned on him, was a good hundred miles away from Thermopylae. Even with a swift horse, it would take him several days to reach Attica. Indeed, it would take him a good three hours just to get down from the mountaintop on which he now stood.

It was therefore a most fortunate thing that that Creator who ordains the rise and fall of all nations whether they know him or not had built into the mind of Alex, as he had into the minds of all men, that most strange and wondrous power of association. By this power can a boy become a king: for all boys like baseball, and in baseball balls are thrown, and thrown sounds like throne, and a king sits on a throne.

As Alex stood alone and afraid peering down on the battlefield that lay a thousand feet below, he thought for a moment of the mountaintop on which he now rested. And as he thought on that, his mind wandered of its own accord to another mountaintop in the state of Tennessee where a man named Davy Crockett would one day be born. And as he thought on that, he began to whistle the tune of "The Ballad of Davy Crockett." And as he whistled that well-loved tune, his mind wandered again to the battle of the Alamo, where he and Stacey had first met Hercules and had been lifted high into the air in preparation for their journey back in time.

"Of course," shouted Alex, "it wasn't the magic of Hercules that caused us to rise into the air above the Alamo, but the valor of the men who died to set Texas free. If the bravery and self-sacrifice of Davy Crockett, Jim Bowie, and all the others could give us the power to fly, then surely the selfless courage of Leonidas and the three-hundred Spartans should give me the same power now." Alex stopped suddenly. He felt sure in his heart that he was right, but he felt equally sure that there was only one way to test his theory.

With slow, deliberate steps, the descendant of Hercules and Leonidas walked to the edge of the cliff. Normally, Alex prided himself on being a logical, rational thinker who only took risks when they were necessary, but as he gazed down on the valley far below, all thoughts of reason and logic fled from his mind. What was needed now was that special kind of courage that is born of hope, those crazy, child-like eyes of faith that can see the magic that runs rampant all around us. What was needed, in short, was a miracle.

Why he did it, he would never know; how he convinced himself to do it, he would never be able to say. All that matters is that he did it. In the face of all logic and reason, Alex threw himself off the cliff. As his body plummeted to earth, he cried out with the full force of his lungs a single word: freedom! The word echoed off the mountains and reverberated in the valley below. The air grew thick with it, and all the clouds froze in the sky. For eight-hundred feet Alex fell, until the grass of the valley lay but a mere two-hundred feet beneath him.

But that was as far as he fell.

A mighty breeze from the battlefield of Thermopylae rose up and over the mountaintop from which Alex had thrown himself. Like two great arms, the breeze stretched downward and caught the falling Alex before his feet could touch the ground. Suspended in the center of the breeze, Alex was lifted swiftly upward until he came to rest three-thousand feet above the valley floor. Then the breeze shifted, and Alex felt his body being propelled forward at a tremendous speed. He did not have to ask in which direction he was moving.

He was on his way to Athens.

✦ ✦ ✦

When Alex landed, two hours later, in the agora of Athens, he found that the city had changed greatly in appearance. Most of the houses had been boarded up, and the Acropolis itself was surrounded on all sides by makeshift barricades of wood and stone. Alex could see at once that these quick defenses would never be able to hold back the Persian army, but this did not seem to dissuade the Athenians from their feverish attempts to secure the city. Indeed, in the midst of the chaos of preparation, Alex saw only one figure who did not seem out of his mind with fear and worry. The figure, of course, was that of Themistocles, he whom the Oracle had once called a most unlikely savior.

"Themistocles," cried Alex, "I have come with news from Thermopylae."

"Do my eyes deceive me," said Themistocles, "or are you the young man with whom I spoke at Delphi? Are you not one of two who helped me to discover the answer to the Oracle's riddle?"

"Yes, Themistocles, it is I. I have come here by order of Leonidas to tell you that the pass has fallen to the Persians and that they will surely reach Athens by the third day, if not sooner. But tell me, have you convinced your fellow citizens yet to abandon their city and flee to Salamis? And have you been able to unite the rest of Greece against Persia?"

"I have tried, child of the Oracle, but I have only partly succeeded. In the second task, I have been more successful than the first. Greece now stands united in her resistance, but my own people are unwilling to do their share. They care only for their homes and their property and refuse to leave the city. Perhaps you can convince them where I have failed."

"I shall do my best," said Alex.

That was all that Themistocles needed to hear. In less than thirty minutes, he gathered together the full assembly of the people and brought them before Alex—who by now had positioned

The Wooden Walls

himself in his favorite spot beneath the statues of Harmodius and Aristogeiton. "Citizens," he said, when all were gathered before him, "I have come to you fresh from the pass of Thermopylae. There I saw a marvelous thing. Three-hundred Spartans whose homes lie far to the south sacrificed their lives for the freedom of their countrymen. They did not think of themselves or their possessions when they met Xerxes on the battlefield. They thought only of how their deaths might serve the interests of all Greece.

"I am sure that there are many of you here today who think, as I once thought, that freedom is a thing that can stand on its own. That you have only to go about your business and let freedom take care of itself. But freedom cannot exist in such a vacuum. It can only exist and thrive when it is shielded on all sides by the four virtues: wisdom, justice, courage, and self-control. Your great founder, Solon, knew this truth as did Peisistratus and Miltiades and all those who died at Marathon. Themistocles knows it as well and has tried in vain to teach it to you.

"All of you here wish to see Athenian freedom survive the invasion of Xerxes. But how can this be? Wisdom tells you that you cannot defend Athens from the Persian army, but must trust to your fleet that awaits you at Salamis. Justice insists that you must make the same sacrifices that you have asked the other city-states of Greece to make. Courage demands that you chose the more difficult way if it will increase your chance to defeat Xerxes. And self-control cries out in the agora that your homes can be rebuilt and your possessions remade, but your honor, once dead, can never be revived. It is only in the midst of these four virtues that freedom will be won; if you forsake them, that same freedom will be ripped from you as the vulture rips the heart from a dead lion.

"Which of you then will heed the true meaning of the Oracle's riddle and cling to the wooden walls of the great navy that Themistocles has built for you? It is not yet too late to decide. Time is still your ally."

Alex ceased speaking, and at once a rousing cry rose up from the crowd. Alex had won their hearts and reminded them of their true inheritance. He had revealed to them the secret of the wooden walls, but it was the four walls of wisdom, justice, courage, and self-control that had spoken to them with even greater eloquence. By the following morning, three quarters of the citizens had strapped what belongings they could to their backs and were prepared to leave for Salamis. There were still many who stayed, most of them old men who refused to leave the Acropolis they had built, but those who left were enough to man the ships and to afford Athens the hope both of victory for Greece and another generation for the city of Athena.

✦ ✦ ✦

When, on the third day after the fall of Thermopylae, Alex reached Salamis with Themistocles and his fellow citizens, he thought to himself that surely now his labors on behalf of Greek freedom would be over. But there was one last task yet to be completed.

"Alex," said Themistocles, when the two were alone together, "thanks to your help, our fleet stands ready in the harbor to meet Xerxes and his navy. Only one problem remains. How are we to convince Xerxes to sail his ships into the narrow straits of Salamis? Xerxes is no fool; he must know that his larger, heavier ships will be less able to maneuver than our own sleeker vessels. If we are to catch the Persian fish, we must bait our hook well."

The Wooden Walls

"What do you have in mind, Themistocles?" asked Alex

"Xerxes is a wise ruler, but his hatred and his ignorance of the ways of freedom are his weakness. As you yourself have told me, he delayed his attack on Thermopylae for four days, because he could not conceive of the idea that free men would be willing to perish in a battle that they could not win. Even so, he does not understand how a democracy can compel its citizens to follow the laws when it lacks dictators and can even send in to exile its own past leaders. He has witnessed the betrayal of men like Hippias and Demaratus and Ephialtes, and he thinks therefore that any man will betray his city-state for the promise of wealth and power. He does not know that there are loyalties that run deeper than gold, that even one like Demaratus can hear again the call of virtue and freedom."

"I think I see what you have in mind," said Alex, "If it were done in the right way, it just might be possible to convince Xerxes that you, Themistocles, are prepared to betray Athens into his hands for the sake of a royal reward."

"Exactly!" said Themistocles, "Alex, I hate to ask another favor of you, but Xerxes already knows you and perhaps even trusts you somewhat. You must go to him at once and tell him that I, Themistocles, am tired of Athenian democracy with its squabbles and its petty laws. It is my hidden desire to destroy the democracy of Athens and put myself in the role of dictator. Tell Xerxes, then, that if he will promise to give me Athens to rule as I see fit that I will deliver to him our entire fleet. Tell him that I will find a way to bottle up every Greek ship in the straits of Salamis. Once there, they will be trapped in the narrow waters and will be unable to escape. The Persian fleet has only to sail into the straits in full force, and they can rid themselves of any further threat from the Greeks."

"It's a brilliant plan," said Alex, "and I think it has another advantage to it. Every hour that we delay, the united Greeks will grow more restless and frightened. If we wait too long to fight, some may abandon the cause and return to their city-states. The Greeks must be made to fight now while their courage and resolve are at their highest."

"You amaze me, boy," said Themistocles, "your cunning is almost as great as my own. You read my thoughts perfectly. These Greeks are a difficult people to hold together. We have a saying in Athens that if you get two Greeks together, you will end up with three different opinions. That is what I have been fighting against for the last year as I've tried my best to hold this shaky coalition together. If we don't strike now, it may all fall apart. Oh yes, it is a dangerous gamble, I know, but I'm afraid it is our only hope."

"Say no more, Themistocles. I will gladly volunteer to carry your message to Xerxes. But does anyone know his current position?"

"Alas," said Themistocles, "I know too well where he is. The news came only an hour ago. The Persians have taken Athens and have burned every building on the Acropolis. If we had stayed, we too would have been killed. Salamis is truly our last hope."

❖ ❖ ❖

Late that evening, weary from riding and sick at heart at the thought of Athens' fate, Alex arrived in the ruins of what had once been the agora. It did not take long before he was dragged before Xerxes by a group of suspicious guards.

"So," said Xerxes, when he recognized who it was that stood before him, "you have returned. Perhaps it would have been better for you if you had not. I am not in the habit of treating deserters with mercy."

"Your majesty," said Alex, "I did not desert you. I have spent the last ten days spying on the Greeks and gathering information for you and your troops. The reason I have returned now is that I have vital news that promises to secure a complete Persian victory by the end of the day tomorrow."

"Tell me this news," said Xerxes, "and I may yet spare your life."

"Lord Xerxes," said Alex, "that is the very purpose for which I have come. For the last several days I have watched carefully the movements of Themistocles the Athenian. When I left your camp ten days ago, it was my plan to try to turn Leonidas the Spartan to the side of Persia, but my attempts all failed. So bewitched was he by the phantom of freedom that he would be satisfied with nothing but his own reckless death. So be it if that was his goal. But this Themistocles is a different matter. He is shrewd and ambitious and knows the way the wind blows. He has heard of your glory and of the might of Persia, and he wishes to link his fate with your own rising star."

"Ha!" said Xerxes, "exactly as I thought. This freedom and democracy of which you Greeks boast is nothing but a sham and an illusion. No man of power and foresight would put himself in the hands of the people or allow himself to be bound by the same laws as the rabble he rules. Your whole foolish experiment was doomed from the start. It is the way of things that the most powerful should rule: so has it been; so shall it ever be."

"Themistocles explained it to me," said Alex, "in words very similar to your own. In return, then, for the dictatorship of Athens, Themistocles has agreed to put in your hands the entire Greek fleet. Take his offer, O king, and by this time tomorrow you will be the lord of all Europe. Even now, Themistocles has used his influence to trick the Greeks into bottling up all of their ships in the narrow straits of Salamis. If you order your own fleet to sail there at once, you can catch the Greeks off guard and destroy their navy in one fell swoop."

"You have done well, child of Delphi," said Xerxes, "I shall give this Themistocles what he desires and shall reward you as well for your service."

"I thank you, king," said Alex, "but for the moment, I have only one desire."

"Name it, and it is yours, even to the half of my kingdom."

"I would like to ascend the Acropolis alone and see for myself the great victory of your army. From there, I must return to Delphi to consult with the Oracle. It is possible that you will see me again, but if you do not, I feel certain that you shall be visited by my sister when you return to Persia. I hope that you will be kind to her for my sake. As for you, my lord, I only wish that you will get the reward you deserve when you descend upon the Greek fleet at Salamis. I think it shall prove a day the world will never forget."

"That it shall, child of the Oracle," said Xerxes, "that it shall."

✦ ✦ ✦

When Alex had reached the summit of the scarred and naked Acropolis, and when he knew for certain that he could not be seen, he fell to his knees and wept for the destruction of the once noble city of Athens.

"What then shall remain?" he cried, "Even if Themistocles wins the battle tomorrow and the Persians are driven out of Greece, what is to become of Athens and her dream of freedom?"

"Do not think, my son, that because the invader has torn down my temple that Athens will never rise again. You say that nothing remains, but you are wrong. Lift up your eyes and behold."

"Athena," said Alex softly, "I had hoped you would meet me here. That's why I asked to be alone. But your words offer little consolation to my heart. What could possibly remain on this citadel of death and decay? Still, since you ask it of me, I will look."

Slowly and with a heavy spirit, Alex lifted up his head and opened his eyes. He expected to see only a pile of charred ruins, but his gaze fell upon something far different. There before him, choked in on all sides by jagged stones and shattered pottery, was Athena's olive tree.

"Yes," said Athena, "my tree has survived, and with it the heart and soul of Athens. The dream has not died. A remnant will survive, and they will rebuild what was torn down."

"But I will keep for myself seven thousand who have not bowed their knee to Baal," said Alex under his breath.

"What is that you are saying, Alex?"

"Oh nothing, Athena, just something I read once in a book. I had forgotten it until now. I had forgotten that when the tree is cut down, the stump remains. And if it remains, it may flourish once again."

"Exactly," said Athena, "just so the seed must die and be buried before it can bear fruit. But come, Alex, I can see that you are weary and in need of rest. You have accomplished the task for which you were brought back to Greece. Now you must ascend with me one last time. There is someone, I think, who longs to meet with you in the air."

Chapter

28

The Golden Age

I do not think I exaggerate when I say that no brother has ever been more overjoyed to see his sister than Alex was when he looked ahead in the sky and saw Stacey lying on a fleecy cloud beside the noble figure of Hercules.

"Stacey," called out Alex in a loud voice, "have you done it? Did you speak with Esther and convince her to save the Jews?"

"I did, Alex, I did," said Stacey, leaping up from the cloud and dancing up and down on the air, "Esther was so beautiful and so brave as well. What about you, did Leonidas listen?"

"He did, Stacey, and he and all his men went to their deaths for freedom. Their courage was amazing and beautiful at the same time."

"What do you think, Athena?" said Hercules, "Have these children performed well or have they not?"

"Hercules, son of Zeus and my own dear half-brother," said Athena, "you have chosen well in bringing these children back to Greece. Truly they are your descendants and those of Leonidas."

"Hercules," said Alex with a broad smile, "I think it's time we went home."

"All in good time, Alex," said Hercules, "all in good time. But don't you wish first to see the fruit of what you and your sister have sown?"

"I do indeed, Hercules," said Alex, "but is it possible."

"You two have *made* it possible. You have set history back on its proper course and secured the triumph of freedom. It will begin tomorrow with the Greek victory at Salamis. Yes, Alex," said Hercules, interpreting the expression on his face, "Xerxes will follow your advice and sail his fleet into the straits. There they will be met and destroyed by the faster, lighter, more maneuverable ships of Themistocles. Xerxes will watch the battle from on high seated on a golden throne, but the sight will bring him no joy. Shortly after the defeat of his navy, a rumor will come to him that the Greeks have sailed to the Hellespont to destroy his bridge and thus leave his army stranded in Greece. In fear, Xerxes will flee back to Persia, never to return. What remains of his forces will wage one last battle against Greece at the city of Plateae (pla TEE ah), but this battle too they shall lose."

"And what of Athens?" said Alex, "Will she rebuild her city?"

"Look below you," said Hercules, "and you will see."

The Golden Age

Alex and Stacey turned their gaze earthward and found that although they were hovering half a mile above the city, they could see every detail of it with perfect clarity and precision.

"What happened to Athens, Alex?" said Stacey who did not yet know that the Persians had sacked the city and burnt every building on the Acropolis.

With a slight tinge of anger in his voice, Alex began to tell Stacey about the whole course of Xerxes' invasion, but before he could reach the part when the Persians took Athens, he saw to his surprise that something was happening on the Acropolis. Workers were swarming all over it like ants on an anthill. They were building, building, but at a phenomenal pace. It was a strange sight, indeed, like watching a movie played at ten times the speed.

"Yes," said Athena, "I have accelerated the normal course of time that you might see what is to come in my beloved city. Within fifty years of Thermopylae and Salamis, Athens will move forward into her Golden Age. Her city will become the envy of the world, and poets, artists, and thinkers from around the globe will flock here in droves. Those disciplines that you call drama, philosophy, ethics, and history will be born here while the arts of painting, rhetoric, sculpture, science, geometry, and architecture will all reach their prime. Here civilization shall have its great and glorious dawn, and its golden rays will stretch out to illuminate, in time, all the nations of the world."

"But what of the Jews?" said Stacey, "What will become of them?"

"They too shall thrive," said Hercules, "and shall keep their religion and their culture alive. Other Hamans will rise to threaten their existence, but the example set by Esther shall be followed by others. So shall they continue for five-hundred years, until that long-awaited time arrives when the western civilization of Athens shall reach out her arms to embrace the eastern religion of the Jews. And when that time comes, the Magi will remember the riddle you gave them, Alex. A man named Balthazar, twentieth in descent from the Balthazar you met at Susa, shall lead his fellow Magi on a long search that shall bring them to a stable in Bethlehem and a child in a manger. There, in that stable, the twin paths of east and west, Jew and Greek shall converge and become one. The manger shall prove a new omphalos, and on it the descendants of Leonidas and Esther shall ride together to glory. There too shall man learn at last how to be truly, fully free: not just from the enemy without but from the darkness and hatred that lurk within.

"But now, Alex, the time *has* come for you and your sister to return. Do not worry. Your absence has not been noticed. Though you did not know it, while you struggled here to keep open the twin gates of freedom, the people of your time were frozen in a state of suspension. By your deeds, you have unthawed them and restored the lifeblood to your civilization. You no longer need my magic or that of Athena to guide you home. The magic now lies within you both. Your eyes have been opened, and you cannot miss your way."

Alex, Stacey, Hercules, and Athena all fell silent for a moment and gazed down at the renewed Acropolis of Athens. Then there was a time of much hugging and kissing and the saying of long goodbyes. When they all had had their fill, Hercules pointed out to the children the pathway that cut through the sky, and Alex and Stacey set off on their journey home. They spoke of many things as they walked, mostly about what they would do first when they returned to Houston.

"I'll tell you what I can't wait to do," said Alex, "I can't wait to tell Daddy that he is a direct descendant of Hercules."

"Don't you think he knows already?" said Stacey.

"Well, he's probably felt it in his heart, but I don't think he ever dreamed it could be true. What about you, Stacey? What do you want to do when you get back?"

"The first thing I'm going to do, Alex, is tell my choir teacher that we have to put on the Esther musical again."

"Why do you want to do that, Stacey?"

"Isn't it obvious, Alex? When they see how well I know the story, they're sure to let me play the part of Esther. Then I'll get to wear the prettiest dresses."

"Stacey," said Alex, "you are one crazy girl!"

About the Author

LOUIS MARKOS holds a BA in English and history from Colgate University and an MA and PhD in English from the University of Michigan. He is a professor of English and scholar-in residence at Houston Christian University, where he holds the Robert H. Ray Chair in Humanities and teaches courses on British Romantic and Victorian poetry, the classics, C. S. Lewis and J. R. R. Tolkien, and art and film. He speaks widely for classical Christian schools and conferences and has authored 28 books, including *From Achilles to Christ: Why Christians Should Read the Pagan Classics*, *On the Shoulders of Hobbits: The Road to Virtue with Tolkien and Lewis*, *The Myth Made Fact: Reading Greek and Roman Mythology through Christian Eyes*, *From Plato to Christ: How Platonic Thought Shaped the Christian Faith*, *Ancient Voices: An Insider's Look at Classical Greece*, *From Aristotle to Christ*, and *Passing the Torch: An Apology for Classical Christian Education*. To see all his books, visit his amazon author page: https://www.amazon.com/author/louismarkos

He has produced two lecture series with The Great Courses, published 350 book chapters, essays, and reviews, and given well over 300 public lectures in over two dozen states as well as Rome, Oxford, Ontario, and British Columbia. He is committed to the concept of the Professor as Public Educator and believes that knowledge must not be walled up in the Academy but must be disseminated to all who have ears to hear. His son Alex teaches ancient history at a classical Christian school near San Antonio, TX; his daughter Stacey teaches music at a classical charter school near Dallas, TX.

About the Illustrator

ANGELA MERKLE has long had a passion for writing and illustrating fantastic worlds and characters. At Houston Christian University, she received a Bachelor of Arts in Art and Writing and a Master of Fine Arts in Creative Writing. She has worked as a graphic designer in the print industry where she designed many logos, signs, car wraps, and window displays. She has also been commissioned to illustrate a number of book covers and internal illustrations. She now works full time as Editor and Communications Coordinator for the Office of the President at Houston Christian University where she employs her artistic talents for invitations, social media posts, and email greetings.

Angela lives in Sugar Land, Texas near her parents, siblings, and nieces and nephews. More examples of her work can be seen on her website, www.angelamerkleart.com.

ALSO AVAILABLE FROM LAMPION HOUSE PUBLISHING

LOOK FOR THESE AND OTHER GREAT TITLES AT:
LAMPIONHOUSEPUBLISHING.COM

LAMPION
House Publishing

www.ingramcontent.com/pod-product-compliance
Lightning Source LLC
Chambersburg PA
CBHW070140100426
42743CB00013B/2772